The Beginner's Guide
to Playing Guitar

The Beginner's Guide
to Playing Guitar

A Simple, A–to–Z Guide
for First-Time Musicians

DOUGLAS J. NOBLE

THE LYONS PRESS
GUILFORD, CONNECTICUT
AN IMPRINT OF THE GLOBE PEQUOT PRESS

HERITAGE PUBLIC LIBRARY
P.O BOX 8
PROVIDENCE FORGE, VA 23140

Dedication

This book is dedicated to all my pupils, many of whom
have worked through the material contained in this book.

Copyright © 2004 by Douglas J. Noble

ALL RIGHTS RESERVED. No part of this book may be reproduced or transmitted in any
form by any means, electronic or mechanical, including photocopying and recording, or
by any information storage and retrieval system, except as may be expressly permitted in
writing from the publisher. Requests for permission should be addressed to The Lyons
Press, Attn: Rights and Permissions Department, P.O. Box 480, Guilford, CT 06437.

The Lyons Press is an imprint of The Globe Pequot Press

10   9   8   7   6   5   4   3   2   1

Printed in the United States of America

Designed byTwoSistersDesign.com

Library of Congress Cataloging-in-Publication Data

Noble, Douglas J.
    The beginner's guide to playing guitar : a simple A–Z guide for first-time musicians /
Douglas J. Noble.
        p. cm.
        Discography: p.
        Includes index.
        ISBN 1-59228-276-8 (pbk.)
Guitar—Methods—Self-instruction. I. Title.

MT588.N63 2004
787.87'193—dc22

                                                            2004042969

Contents

Introduction

The purpose of this book is to enable a reader with no prior knowledge of the guitar and no prior musical knowledge to learn the basics of how to play the guitar. The eagle-eyed among you will notice that there is no CD or tape with this book—that's because there is no need for one! All the musical examples included in this book are suitable for the total beginner and hence the timing has been kept straightforward.

There are some "actual songs" in the book but most of the material is written specifically to improve a certain aspect of one's playing, and this is often best served with a specific exercise rather than, for example, a well-known song. The reader will work progressively through a variety of different styles in the book—the guitar readily lends itself to many different styles of music. Even if you are not particularly interested in jazz, for example, the jazz chapter is still worth working through, since it covers playing techniques and theory that can be applied to other types of music. No one style of music exists in total isolation from other styles.

It is very important to take your time and play all the musical examples very slowly at first. How many guitarists does it take to change a light bulb? Five—one to screw in the bulb and four to say they could have done it faster. Beginners (and even some advanced guitarists!) often make the mistake of trying to play too fast, which is ironic since the guitar is a particularly difficult instrument to play fast.

Beginners often worry whether or not they are progressing at the proper rate. Worry not! Everyone will progress at different rates. The important thing is to practice a little—that is, ten to fifteen minutes—every day rather than a lot one day and not at all for the next three days. This book stresses the importance of good technique; when self-taught players go to lessons (and I'm speaking from personal experience here!) they usually have to unlearn bad habits because they didn't realize they were doing something wrong. We'll also look at some basic theory relevant to the guitar.

Are you ready? Then let us begin!

Chapter 1

Getting Started

Why Play Guitar?

The guitar is one of the most versatile of musical instruments. It can be used to play a huge variety of musical styles such as folk, country, blues, rock, pop, jazz, classical, and flamenco, and can be played either solo or with other people.

Many beginners ask whether the guitar is easier or harder to learn than other instruments. While all instruments have their peculiarities and idiosyncrasies, at a basic level it is fairly easy to produce a musical sound from the guitar. At first base it is easier than, say, a violin, which requires precise fingering, considerable coordination between the hands, and a good ear, but the guitar is arguably harder than, for example, the piano, where the actual mechanics of producing a musical note are done for you after depressing a piano key.

After covering the basics, playing the guitar is as difficult as you want to make it. It depends how proficient you want to become in your chosen style. Once the basic open chords have been learned and some simple accompaniment techniques developed, the guitarist can play many folk, country, blues, rock, and pop songs. However, within each of these styles there are many guitarists who have taken their craft much further and play at a very high level of technical proficiency (see Chapter 13, Discography, for recommended listening in different musical genres).

Classical guitar and flamenco guitar have the most disciplined and traditional approaches to technique—that is, there is a prescribed way to sit, a way to hold the guitar and a way to use the fingers of both hands. Both the classical guitar and the flamenco guitar—the guitar used in flamenco is slightly different from the classical guitar—are relatively quiet instruments, and as the classical guitarist Julian Bream once poetically remarked, the note is dying away as soon as the player has plucked the string. In effect, it is a challenge to project either a classical or flamenco guitar's sound to an audience.

This book stresses the importance of good technique from the very beginning, regardless of musical style. Good technique enables the guitarist to play to the best of his or her ability with the minimum of effort. Playing with minimum effort does not suggest laziness—good technique involves eliminating unnecessary finger movements in order to lessen the likelihood of making a mistake and to conserve energy. Good technique also minimizes the risk of giving oneself an injury: guitarists who practice for too long or use poor hand positions can develop strains in the wrist that are difficult to eradicate. In the longer term, it is a good idea to get a teacher to check that your technique is correct. There are a lot of aspects to get right and a good teacher's insight can be invaluable.

Beginner, intermediate, and advanced guitarists can always learn from watching other players, but be wary of adopting unconventional posture, hand positions, and fingerings from other players: what works for one player might not necessarily be the right approach for another. By following the basic principles laid out in this book, the beginner is sure to stay on the correct track.

Choosing a Guitar

There are three main kinds of guitar: a classical or Spanish guitar (these two terms essentially mean the same thing), an acoustic guitar, and an electric guitar. The term "acoustic guitar" is often used to refer to any guitar which is not an electric guitar, but more properly speaking a distinction must be drawn between nylon-string classical or Spanish guitars and steel-strung acoustic guitars. Classical guitars are, as the name obviously suggests, played by classical guitarists such as John Williams, Julian Bream, and Segovia, and have nylon-based strings—the highest sounding three strings are nylon only and

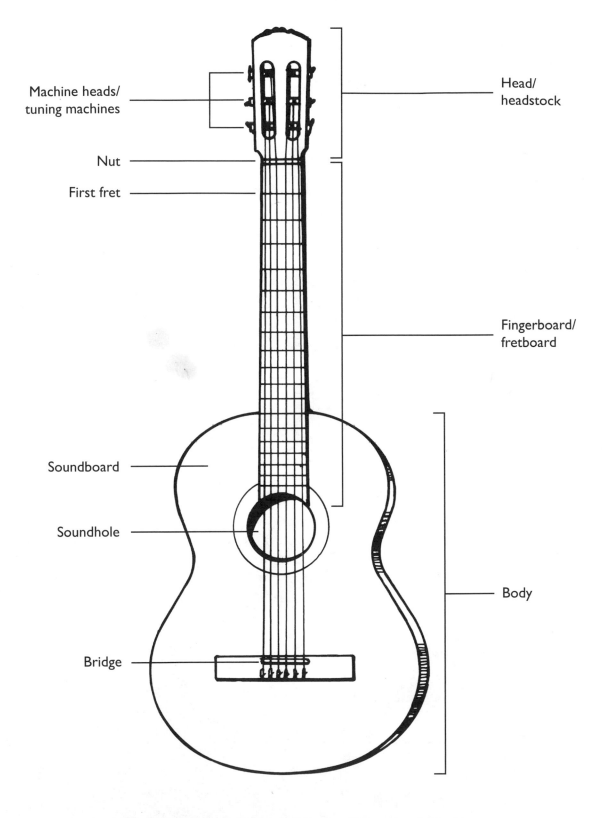

Machine heads/
tuning machines

Head/
headstock

Nut

First fret

Fingerboard/
fretboard

Soundboard

Soundhole

Body

Bridge

The Different Parts of the Classical Guitar

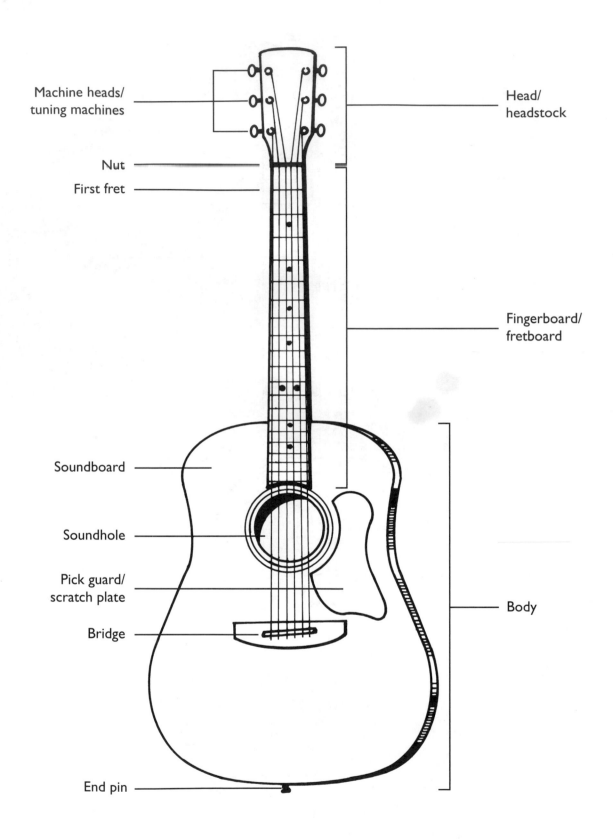

Machine heads/
tuning machines

Nut

First fret

Soundboard

Soundhole

Pick guard/
scratch plate

Bridge

End pin

Head/
headstock

Fingerboard/
fretboard

Body

The Different Parts of the Acoustic Guitar

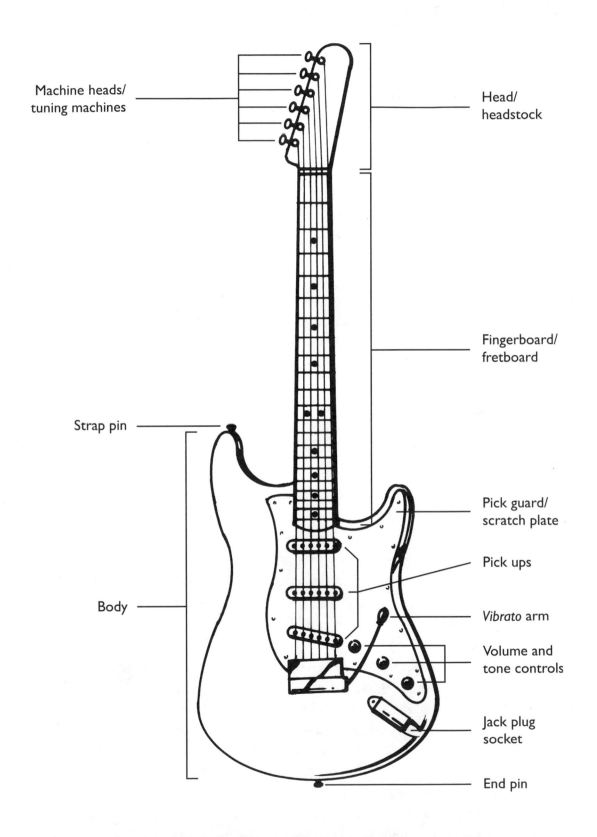

Machine heads/
tuning machines

Head/
headstock

Fingerboard/
fretboard

Strap pin

Pick guard/
scratch plate

Pick ups

Body

Vibrato arm

Volume and
tone controls

Jack plug
socket

End pin

The Different Parts of the Electric Guitar

the lowest three strings are wire-covered nylon strings. Despite its name, a classical guitar is actually suited to the learning of a variety of styles (albeit at a basic level), not just classical, and is the best type of guitar for the beginner to start on—the strings are relatively easy to press onto the fretboard and the wide neck gives your right-hand fingers room to maneuver.

The disadvantages for a beginner learning on an acoustic guitar are that the steel strings can make the fingers very sore until calluses are developed, the narrow neck means finger placement has to be very precise, and the large body size—larger than a classical guitar—can make it difficult to hold. Acoustic guitars are used by folk, country, blues, and rock musicians and have more treble in tone than a classical guitar and produce a louder sound. An acoustic guitar can be heard at the beginning of Led Zeppelin's "Stairway to Heaven," a favorite for guitarists from the '70s, Oasis's "Wonderwall," a popular song for guitarists to strum from the '90s, as well as "Here Comes the Sun" by the Beatles and many Bob Dylan songs such as "Blowin' in the Wind" and "The Times They Are a-Changin'."

The disadvantage of starting on an electric guitar is that an amplifier is also required, making the initial outlay greater than if buying a classical guitar or an acoustic guitar. Prices and package deals vary considerably, but as a very rough guide, an electric guitar with amplifier will cost approximately twice as much as a classical guitar.

Visit a good, reputable music shop that will be only too happy to help you choose a guitar. There are several things to look for when buying a guitar, and a total beginner will lack the necessary experience to make suitable judgments on these things; this is why it is best to go to a reputable music shop rather than buying second-hand. Even better, go to a music shop with a friend who plays the guitar. One of the most important things to look out for is the "action" of the guitar—this is the distance between the fretboard and the strings (see pages 3–5 for a detailed look at the different parts of the guitar). If the action is too high, notes will be difficult to hold down onto the fretboard. If the action is too low, the notes will buzz against the fretboard. The action on an electric guitar is lower than the action on a classical guitar and an acoustic guitar, which makes an electric guitar easier to play as far as fretting notes is concerned.

Check that the machine heads (the pegs used for tuning the guitar) all turn smoothly. Play all the notes on each string from the open string (that is, without any left-hand fingers on it) up to the highest playable fret, making sure all the notes sound clearly. On an electric guitar turn the volume and tone controls and listen for a gradual change, ensuring the controls work correctly. Also check that the pick up selector switch works correctly by listening to the sound of the guitar in each different selector switch position.

A new guitar will obviously cost more than a second-hand guitar but at least you will benefit from the advice and guidance offered by a shop. All the music in this book can be played on either a classical, acoustic, or electric guitar. There is no need to buy an expensive guitar; sounding good has as much to do with how you play and your confidence as with the price tag on the guitar.

At the same time you purchase your guitar you should also buy a soft case (or "gig bag") for the guitar for carrying it around and offering some protection to the instrument. For more expensive guitars a hard case (or "flight case") should perhaps be bought, but for less expensive instruments this is not necessary—a hard case can cost more than an inexpensive guitar!

It is also a good idea to buy an electronic tuner. Traditional methods of tuning the guitar include tuning to a piano, which assumes you have a piano tuned at "concert pitch" (a standard pitch adopted by all instruments), tuning with pitch pipes (which are renowned for producing a terrible tone), or tuning with a tuning fork. All three methods assume the beginner has a good ear. Some people are born with a good ear, others are not; but don't worry. The more you play—and the more you listen—the better your "ear" will develop. (Just like learning to play the guitar, you can learn to develop your ear—there are several examples of what to listen for throughout this book.) It may seem like cheating to use an electronic device to tune the guitar, but for the beginner with no previous musical experience tuning can be a very difficult and discouraging experience.

You should also purchase picks of a variety of thicknesses. Generally, picks come in three thicknesses: thin, medium, and hard. The beginner will probably find thin picks the easiest with which to strum the chords in this chapter; medium picks will produce a better, fuller and louder tone; hard picks (the thickest) produce the clearest articulation when playing single notes.

Generally speaking, intermediate and advanced guitarists favor medium and hard picks.

Finally, it would be useful to buy a bookstand or a music stand to hold this book open when you are playing the various musical examples, since you will obviously need both hands free for playing the guitar!

Left-Handers

A few words for left-handers: James Brown had a fair point when he sang "It's A Man's Man's Man's World"; he would have also been bang on the mark if he had sung "It's A Right, Right, Right-Handed Person's World." The choice of guitar is limited if you are left-handed and they generally cost more than the equivalent right-handed model. Of the three main types of guitar, inexpensive classical guitars can readily be transformed into left-handed guitars just by reversing the strings (more expensive left-handed classical guitars are custom made). Right-handed acoustic and electric guitars do not readily lend themselves to such a transformation, but left-handed beginners' models are produced.

If you write with your left hand, do not automatically assume that you will play guitar left-handed; some left-handers, such as Mark Knopfler, play guitar right-handed and there is a good argument to be made for using one's strong hand (the left hand if you are left-handed) for the part which normally does the most work (that is, on the fretboard), which would be equivalent to a left-hander playing what we regard as right-handed. However, this would suggest that right-handers should play what we regard as the left-handed way, so let's not pursue this argument!

The guitar is almost the only instrument that the player can play either right- or left-handed. For most instruments, players have to learn specialized and difficult tasks for both hands, so it is taken that it doesn't matter whether the player is right- or left-handed. Hence, there is a school of thought that says everyone should learn the same way; that is, in the manner perceived to be the right-handed way. For orchestral instruments such as the violin, there are additional practical and aesthetic considerations: the layout of an orchestra would be more complicated if there was a mixture of left- and right-handed players with players having to make sure they didn't accidentally elbow anyone in the face and, visually, the uniformity of everyone playing the same way would be spoiled. Perhaps related to this traditional classical way of thinking, there are very few left-handed classical guitarists, but in the world of rock music—in which anything goes, basically—there have been many prominent left-handed players such as Jimi Hendrix, Paul McCartney, and Kurt Cobain.

Since not even classical guitarists have to conform to the layout of the orchestra—the classical guitar is not part of the orchestra—we can dispense with the "fascism" of everyone playing right-handed. However, if, as a left-hander, you feel equally comfortable playing right-handed, then you would be well advised to play right-handed for the greater choice of guitars this gives. Tuition books are almost without fail written for right-handers, both in chord diagrams and text; however, this is easy enough to adjust to. As a left-hander myself, I have written this book assuming the reader is playing right-handed.

The Names of the Open Strings
The names of the open (unfretted) strings, starting from the thickest (or lowest sounding) string, are: E, A, D, G, B, E. A convenient (if rather nonsensical) mnemonic is "Elephants And Dogs Get Biology Exams," the initial letter of each word giving the letter names of the strings, starting from the bottom string. The lowest sounding string—the thickest string—is referred to as the bottom string; the highest sounding string—the thinnest string—is referred to as the top string. Beginners often confuse "top" and "bottom" string, thinking the bottom string is the one nearest the ground and the top string is the one nearest the player's head; just remember, "top" and "bottom" refer to *pitch,* that is, whether the string sounds high or low.

A string is often indicated by a number in a circle (see sample chord diagram on page 12).

Relative Tuning Method
Whatever type of guitar you play, it should be tuned before you practice—ideally, this means every day! A guitar with new strings will go out of tune for perhaps a couple of weeks until the strings settle—new strings will stretch causing the pitch of the strings to go flat (or lower in pitch). Changes in temperature will also cause strings to go out of tune, so try to keep the guitar where the temperature is relatively constant—not too hot and not too cold.

The relative tuning method enables one to tune the guitar so it will be in tune with itself, though not necessarily at the correct pitch overall unless one has something to tune either the top or bottom string to, such as a tuning fork to give A on the top string 5th fret.

Assuming you don't have something to use as a reference note, start with the bottom string since this is likely to vary less in pitch than the top string. Assume the bottom string is at the correct pitch. Then:

Play the bottom string at the 5th fret. Tune the open 5th string to this note using the machine head.

Play the 5th string at the 5th fret. Tune the open 4th string to this note.

Play the 4th string at the 5th fret. Tune the open 3rd string to this note.

Play the 3rd string at the 4th fret. Tune the open 2nd string to this note.

Play the 2nd string at the 5th fret. Tune the open 1st string to this note.

If you have a tuning fork to tune the top string to, this procedure is followed in reverse.

It is important to distinguish between tone and pitch. For example, when your guitar is in tune play the 3rd string at the 9th fret, listen closely to the note, then play the top string open. These two pitches are both E but there is a difference in *tone;* the note on the 3rd string 9th fret has a thicker tone with slightly more bass, partly because it is being played on a thicker string and partly because it is being played relatively high up the fretboard. The open E has a lighter tone with more treble because it is played on a thinner string and it also has a more resonant quality because it is an open string.

Using a Tuner

While it is obviously a very useful skill to be able to tune the guitar by ear (as in the Relative Tuning Method above), most beginners find it difficult and it can take weeks or even longer before a beginner can tune the guitar accurately and quickly by ear. A common alternative is to use an electronic tuner. Some may see this as "cheating" but it is undeniably preferable to spend three minutes with a tuner than, say, thirty minutes struggling to tune by ear. Besides speed, another advantage of using a tuner is that the guitar can be kept at exactly the same pitch, which will in itself help the strings stay in tune.

All tuners come with a set of instructions but the basic procedure is more or less the same. If tuning an acoustic or classical guitar the microphone on the tuner picks up the sound, so place the tuner roughly 10 to 15 centimeters from the guitar's sound hole so it receives a good, strong note. If tuning an electric guitar, the guitar needs to be plugged into the tuner using a conventional guitar lead; make sure the guitar's volume and tone controls are on full so the tuner picks up the strongest possible signal.

Most tuners have two settings: a "guitar" (or "manual") setting and a "chromatic" (or "automatic") setting. On the guitar setting, each string has to be selected in turn by pressing a button on the tuner. On the chromatic setting, the tuner will tell you what note you are playing.

Pluck the string once, firmly. Most tuners have lights and a needle; normally, if the light on the right-hand side lights up, the note is sharp; if the light on the left-hand side lights up, the note is flat. Tune the note using the machine head as appropriate. For fine-tuning, the needle should be in the middle of the display; if the needle is to the right, the note is sharp (higher than it should be); if it's to the left, the note is flat (lower than it should be). Again, tune the note using the machine head as appropriate.

If the guitar is wildly out of tune, some tuners struggle to cope. If you suspect this is the case, the best solution is to take the guitar and tuner back to the friendly, helpful shop where you got it and politely ask them to tune the guitar. Then, provided you regularly tune the guitar, it shouldn't go drastically out of tune again.

Chord Diagrams

Look at the example chord diagram opposite. The fingers of the left hand are numbered 1 to 4, starting with the index finger. So, the index finger is 1, middle finger is 2, ring finger is 3 and pinkie is 4.

If you are left-handed, you have to imagine a mirror image of the right-handed chord diagram—everything is reversed. As

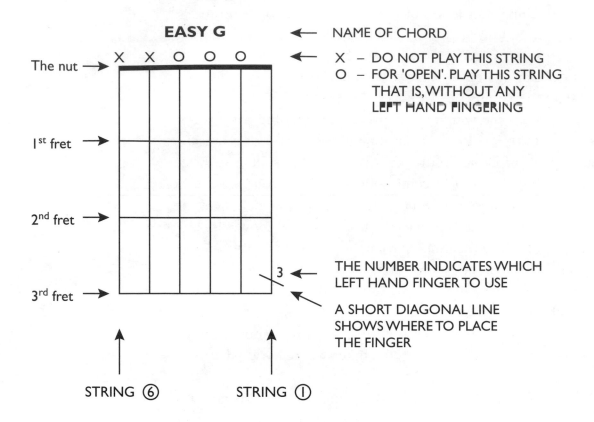

EASY G ← NAME OF CHORD

The nut →   X   X   O   O   O   ←   X – DO NOT PLAY THIS STRING
                                            O – FOR 'OPEN'. PLAY THIS STRING
                                                  THAT IS, WITHOUT ANY
                                                  LEFT HAND FINGERING

1st fret →

2nd fret →

                                    3 ←   THE NUMBER INDICATES WHICH
                                            LEFT HAND FINGER TO USE

3rd fret →   ←   A SHORT DIAGONAL LINE
                                            SHOWS WHERE TO PLACE
                                            THE FINGER

STRING ⑥   STRING ①

already stated, chord diagrams are almost never written for left-handers so you'd better get used to reversing them!

Easy G, Easy G7, and Easy C Chords

These chords have been simplified for the beginner, hence their names which distinguish them from the "proper" versions of these chords. "Easy" simply means that the chords are played with one finger only of the left hand and does not necessarily mean that the reader will whiz through these chords with only the merest application; all musical examples in this book should be approached slowly and methodically, striving to produce a musical sound.

Sit on the edge of a seat of medium height, feet flat on the floor. The hollow part of the body of the guitar should sit on the right thigh. The neck of the guitar should slope gently upwards and the body of the guitar should be at right angles to the ground—this makes it difficult to see the fretboard, but in the longer term we are aiming not to look at the fretboard in order to place the fingers. The back of the guitar should rest against your lower chest.

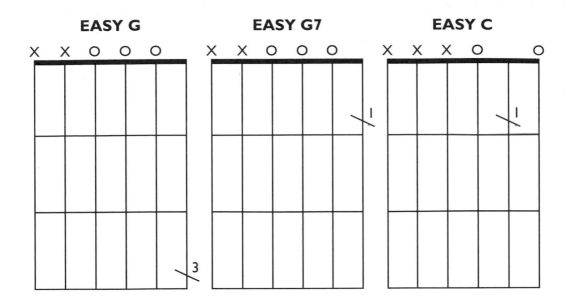

EASY G   EASY G7   EASY C

Press strings against the fretboard with the tips of the fingers—left-hand nails must therefore be kept short. The fingers should be gently curved throughout each of the three joints of the finger. Fingers should be placed immediately behind the frets—not on top of the fret, which will produce a dull sound, and not halfway between the frets, since this will produce a buzzing note.

Fingers should be kept spread out, roughly one-finger-per-fret, even though for these chords only one finger is being used at a time. In the case of the G chord, the left-hand thumb will be roughly behind or opposite the 2nd finger, which will be poised above the 2nd fret. Keep the left-hand fingers that are not being used as close to the fretboard as possible so if and when you do need to use them they are readily available.

Holding down notes on the guitar will hurt the tips of the left-hand fingers for the first couple of weeks or so until the fingertips toughen up and calluses are developed. It is especially important for the beginner to practice regularly—say, 10 minutes a day, at least five days a week. Too much practice and the pain may be off-putting and discouraging; too irregular practice and the fingers won't get a proper chance to toughen up.

Hold a thin or medium pick in the right hand between the thumb and 1st finger with the pointed part towards the strings. Don't hold too tightly. The general rule for both hands is to use the minimum amount of pressure and effort necessary.

Take each of the chords in turn and play through the required number of strings very slowly, one note at a time, and listen to each note produced—we want a good, clear, strong note. Special care must be taken with Easy C—the tip of the 1st finger must be kept upright so that it doesn't touch the 3rd or 1st string. After you have made sure that all of the individual notes in a chord are sounding clearly, take each chord and strum it in turn. To strum a chord, hit the required strings swiftly, moving towards the ground, the end result being that the strings sound (to all practical purposes) simultaneously.

Now we are going to play these chords in a progression. Strum the Easy G chord four times, Easy G7 four times, and Easy C eight times. Then repeat. Written in chord chart notation, this would look like this:

$\frac{4}{4}$ Easy G ////|Easy G7////|Easy C////|Easy C///:||

The two numbers at the beginning of the line are known as the "time signature." The top number tells the number of beats in the bar, which for now also tells us the number of downward strums in the bar. The bottom number of the time signature is not important at this stage and will be tackled in Chapter 2. The vertical lines are bar lines that break the music down into smaller easily digestible parts called "bars."

In the chord chart above, when you see a chord name (for example, Easy G) you strum it once; the forward slash line (/) means strum the same chord again. Therefore, in the first bar you strum the Easy G chord four times altogether; in the second bar you strum the Easy G7 chord four times; in the third and fourth bars you strum the Easy C chord four times, making eight times altogether. The double bar lines at the end of the progression mean the end of a section; the double dots mean repeat from the beginning.

When strumming, take care to strum at the right-hand side of the sound hole as you are looking down on the guitar. The sound box amplifies the sound of the guitar and shapes the tone; if your right hand is in front of the sound hole you will produce a quieter and muffled tone.

Leave a reasonable gap between your strums—most beginners try to play much too quickly. The aim is to get the chord change in time with your strumming so there is no pause between the bars. To encourage this, tap your foot on the beat—four taps to each bar, coinciding with your strumming—and slowly count "one, two, three, four" for each bar (again coinciding with your strumming).

Easy Gmaj7 Chord

The "maj" is short for "major"—so the full name of Easy Gmaj7 is Easy G major 7. This chord may sound strange by itself, but it fits in with the three chords previously learned in the following chord progression.

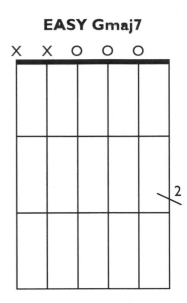

EASY Gmaj7

$\frac{4}{4}$ Easy G///|Easy Gmaj7///|Easy G7///|Easy C///:||Easy G

You should be able to translate this chord chart, but for confirmation it means: strum Easy G four times; strum Easy Gmaj7 four times; strum Easy G7 four times; strum Easy C four times. Repeat from the beginning. Finish with a single strum of Easy G.

Résumé

By now you should have learned the names and numbers of the strings and know which is the "top" string and which is the "bottom" string. You should have also memorized how to tune the guitar using the Relative Tuning Method.

You should practice for 10 minutes a day, at least five days a week—it is better to practice a little each day than a lot one day and not at all for the next two/three days, especially at the beginning. You should memorize the Easy G, Easy G7, Easy C, and Easy Gmaj7 chord shapes and practice changing smoothly between the chords in the two given chord progressions. With a bit of practice you should find that these chords are not particularly difficult; however, it is important to be playing the chords with the correct technique (the correct left-hand position and the correct strumming technique described earlier).

Chapter 2

Guitar Music Notation

The Three Different Kinds of Guitar Music

Generally speaking, there are three main types of guitar books found in music shops, each with their own notation—song arrangement books, classical guitar books, and transcription books.

Song arrangement books are generally scored for piano, voice, and guitar (PVG). That is, the melody of the song is given in music notation with the words, together with an accompaniment for the piano and the corresponding guitar chords. Unlike the chord notation explained in Chapter 1 under Easy G, Easy G7, and Easy C Chords, the player is not told how many times to strum the chords, nor what rhythm to play them in—this is left to the discretion, taste, and experience of the guitarist (assuming we guitarists have any taste, that is!). Beginners are sometimes disappointed when they buy arrangement books because they do not include the guitar riffs, fills, and solos, but simply reduce the guitar part to chord boxes.

Also, beginners can be frustrated by arrangement books because songs are sometimes moved into keys that suit the piano accompaniment but are not guitar-friendly keys. Furthermore, the guitar chord boxes are sometimes not the best voicings for particular chords since they have not been chosen by a guitarist (for more on this see Chapter 9).

Classical guitar music is nearly always written in traditional music notation, that is, on the treble clef with the "dots" representing notes. The ability to play from classical guitar music obviously requires a good, solid understanding of traditional music reading.

Transcription books are note-for-note annotations of songs, often for a particular album/CD. For example, a transcription book for the Beatles' *Abbey Road* will include all the songs from that album with all the guitar parts for each song. These books are usually written in traditional music notation with corresponding tablature.

It is not necessary to be able to read music to play the guitar. However, if you are going to learn from books—and hey, you've bought this one so that's what you're doing right now!—you must at least understand chord diagrams and tablature. (You've presumably completed Chapter 1 so you should understand chord diagrams, and tablature will follow shortly.) However, if you wish to pursue classical guitar or flamenco guitar it is necessary to read music; also, if you wish to study music theory (in order, say, to understand chords more clearly) it is necessary to have a good grasp of how to read music.

Reading Tablature

Tablature is considerably easier to understand and quicker to master than traditional music notation. Tablature is a system of writing music in which six lines represent the six strings of the guitar—the top line (the line nearest the top of the page) stands for the top string (the string that's the highest in pitch) and the bottom line, the line nearest the bottom of the page, stands for the bottom string (the string that sounds the lowest). Numbers are written on lines to tell the guitarist which fret to play; a "0" means an open string, a "1" means play the string at the first fret, etc. The following example shows how the open strings, played from bottom to top string, would look in tablature (denoted by "TAB") below the corresponding music notation—tablature is usually accompanied by traditional music notation.

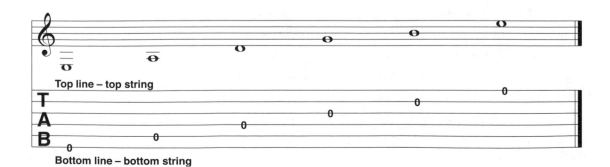

If the numbers are written in a vertical plane, it means play the notes simultaneously as in a chord. The example below shows how the chord progression from Chapter 1's Easy G, Easy G7, and Easy C Chords section would look in tablature.

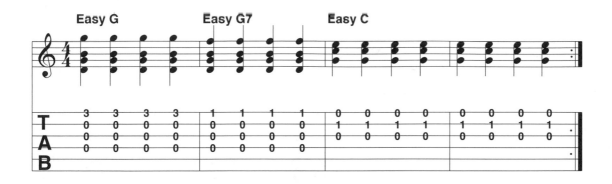

The disadvantage of tablature is that, in its most basic form, it doesn't tell the player how long a note lasts. There are more sophisticated versions of tablature that do tell you how long notes last but they are relatively uncommon and require a grasp of basic traditional music reading principles. The advantage that tablature has over music notation is that it tells you exactly where to play a note. Unlike, for example, the piano, on which there is only one key for every note, on the guitar most notes can be played in more than one place. The note E produced by the open top string can also be played on the 2nd string 5th fret, on the 3rd string 9th fret, on the 4th string 14th fret, and on the 5th string 19th fret.

Music Notation

Classical guitar music is nearly always written solely in traditional music notation. The main advantage music notation has over tablature is that it tells you how long notes last and thus tells you the timing and rhythm for a piece of music. At a more sophisticated level, traditional music notation has two other advantages over tablature. First, the shape of a melody line is immediately apparent from looking at music. For example, the melody may gradually ascend in pitch then quickly descend in pitch. This would be immediately apparent from the shape of the melody in music notation in a way it wouldn't be in tablature. Secondly, from the number and nature of accidentals in the music (that is, notes from outside the song's key) the player can get an idea of the tonality of the music—that is, whether it is going to stick closely to the original key or whether it is going to venture into closely related or even distantly related keys.

The disadvantage of music notation compared with tablature is that it doesn't normally show you where to play a note on the guitar: remember most notes on the guitar can be played in different places. Generally speaking, notes are played in the lowest position, as close to the nut as possible.

The musical examples in this book are all rhythmically straightforward and are written in music notation and tablature in order to make them as accessible as possible. Here we will look at just the basics of reading music—it is possible to write a whole book on reading music for the guitar, and mastering reading music for the guitar takes months of dedicated practice.

Guitarists are notoriously bad music readers compared to other instrumentalists, partly because the guitar is often learned by ear and partly because the guitar has some unique difficulties when learning to read music.

Music Reading Fundamentals

Guitar music is written on a five-lined stave or staff with a treble clef (the "squiggly line" drawn at the beginning of guitar music). The start of the treble clef indicates the position of G on the second to last line of the treble clef. Strictly speaking, for guitar music the treble clef should always have a little "8" written on the bottom to denote that guitar music is written an octave higher than it sounds.

The treble clef is followed by two numbers, which are known as the "time signature." The top number tells you the number of beats in the bar and the bottom number tells you what type of note is being used to represent the beat (the value of each beat). The top number is easy to understand; beginners find the concept behind the bottom number harder to understand and, indeed, it will only be fully understood when the beginner has had some practical experience of different time signatures.

Before we look at how to read music it is useful to appreciate how musical notes are named. Musical notes are named from the first seven letters of the alphabet; A, B, C, D, E, F, G. Each adjacent pair of notes (for example, A and B) has a sharp and a flat note in between them, with two exceptions. For example, play the open 5th string—we already know this note is called A. Play the note at the 1st fret: because this is one fret higher than A, it is called A-sharp which is written as A♯. The note at the 2nd fret is called B, so the note at the 1st fret can also be thought of as being one fret lower than B making it B-flat, written as B♭. Therefore, the note at the 1st fret on the 5th string can have two names—A♯ or B♭.

The two exceptions to this are E and F, which do not have a sharp or flat note between them and B and C, which also do not have a sharp or flat note between them. So, starting on the open 5th string, play the following notes and give them their names:

5th string open—the name of this note is A.

5th string 1st fret—this note can have two names, A♯ because it is one fret higher than A and B♭ because it is one fret lower than B.

5th string 2nd fret—the name of this note is B.

5th string 3rd fret—the name of this note is C (remember, there is no sharp or flat note between B and C).

5th string 4th fret—this note can have two names, C♯ because it is one fret higher than C and D♭ because it is one fret lower than D.

5th string 5th fret—the name of this note is D. Remember back in Chapter 1 in the section entitled Relative Tuning Method you were told that the note on the 5th string 5th fret should be the same as the open 4th string—now you can see for yourself why the 5th string 5th fret is a D note.

5th string 6th fret—this note can have two names, D♯ and E♭.

5th string 7th fret—the name of this note is E.

5th string 8th fret—the name of this note is F (remember, there is no sharp or flat note between E and F).

5th string 9th fret—this note can have two names, F♯ and G♭.

5th string 10th fret—the name of this note is G.

5th string 11th fret—this note can have two names, G♯ and A♭.

5th string 12th fret—the name of this note is A.

Notice how the open string is called A and the 12th fret is also called A. We are back to where we started and if it were possible to play further on your guitar (classical guitars are generally inaccessible above the 12th fret since the body joins the fingerboard at this point) the order of notes would repeat. The distance between these two A notes is called an "octave." This relationship holds for all the open strings—the name of the note at the 12th fret is the same as the name of the open string. Therefore, the distance between any open string and the 12th fret of that string is an octave.

The order of the notes is the same on every string as just played through on the 5th string, but obviously starting on the appropriate open string. Therefore, the first five notes on each of the open strings, starting with the bottom string, are as follows:

On the bottom string:
E, F, F♯/G♭, G, G♯/A♭, etc.

On the 5th string:
A, A♯/B♭, B, C, C♯/D♭, etc.

On the 4th string:
D, D♯/E♭, E, F, F♯/G♭, etc.

On the 3rd string:
G, G♯/A♭, A, A♯/B♭, B, etc.

On the 2nd string:
B, C, C♯/D♭, D, D♯/E♭, etc.

On the top string:
E, F, F♯/G♭, G, G♯/A♭, etc.

We will now look in turn at the two main aspects to reading music—pitch and rhythm.

Reading Music Notation—Pitch

The notes on the lines of the treble clef can be conveniently memorized with the mnemonic "Every Good Boy Deserves Favor (or Football or Fudge)," the initial letter of each word giving the name of the note on each line, starting from the bottom line. For the spaces, the letters in the word "FACE" give the names of the notes in the spaces, starting from the bottom space. The following illustration shows the names of the notes on the lines and in the

spaces and the accompanying tablature shows where these notes
are found on the guitar.

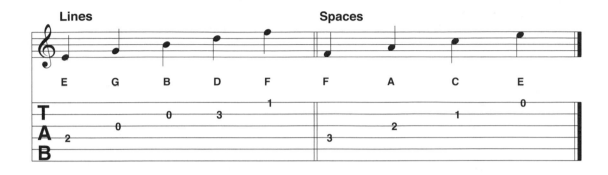

You will notice that this does not account for all the notes on
the guitar. In order to increase the range above and below the
stave, short lines called "ledger lines" are drawn. The following
"note dictionary" shows a diatonic scale (diatonic means it contains
no sharps or flats) starting from the open bottom string. Notice the
direction of the "stems" on the notes—stems always point towards
the middle line of the staff.

Note Dictionary

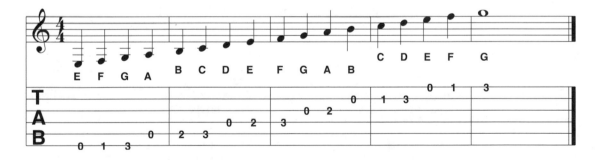

In order to "fill in the gaps" on the fretboard, sharps or flats are
placed in front of the relevant note. The following example shows
how the first five notes on the open top string, moving up one fret
at a time, would be written, first with sharps then with flats. In the
third bar, the last note, a G note, has a natural sign in front of it—
this restores the note to its original pitch and cancels out the flat in
front of the G note immediately to the left of it. Sharps or flats in a
piece of music—known as "accidentals"—last for the whole bar
unless otherwise cancelled.

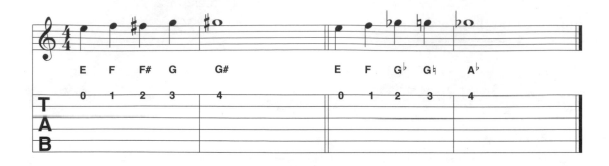

Reading Music Notation—Rhythm

The four main kinds of notes encountered are, starting with the longest note, *semibreve, minim, crotchet,* and *quaver.* These are the European names for the notes; the corresponding American names are whole note, half note, quarter note, and eighth note. In $\frac{4}{4}$ time, the *semibreve*/whole note gets 4 beats, the *minim*/half note gets 2 beats, the *crotchet*/quarter note gets 1 beat, and the *quaver*/eighth note gets half a beat.

A dot placed after a note increases its value by half. For example, a *minim* (worth 2 beats) with a dot after it will be worth 3 beats.

Each note has its own equivalent "rest" symbol that is used to indicate silence, or rather when no note is played.

Shape	European name (American name)	Number of beats in $\frac{4}{4}$ time	Rest shape
o	*Semibreve* (Whole note)	4	
♩	*Minim* (Half note)	2	
♩	*Crotchet* (Quarter note)	I	
♪	*Quaver* (Eighth note)	½	

It is important when learning to read music to tap your foot on the beat and count the beats of the bar aloud. This exercise mixes *semibreves*/whole notes and *minims*/half notes. The beginner's main fault when learning to read music is to play far too fast, so PLAY SLOWLY!

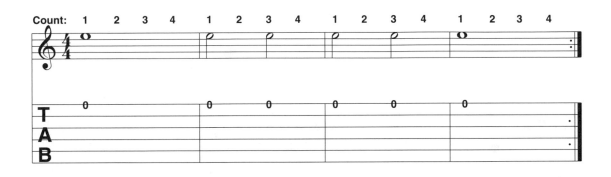

Exercise 1 below mixes *crotchets*/quarter notes and *quavers*/eighth notes. Since the *quavers* receive half a beat it is necessary to count "and" for the *quavers*. Again, play slowly, tap your foot on the beat (do not tap the *quavers'* rhythm when you come to them—stick to the beat), and count aloud.

Exercise 2, on the next page, mixes the four types of notes encountered—*semibreves*/whole notes, *minims*/half notes, *crotchets*/quarter notes, and *quavers*/eighth notes.

Exercise 1

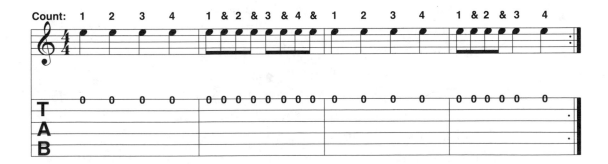

Exercise 2

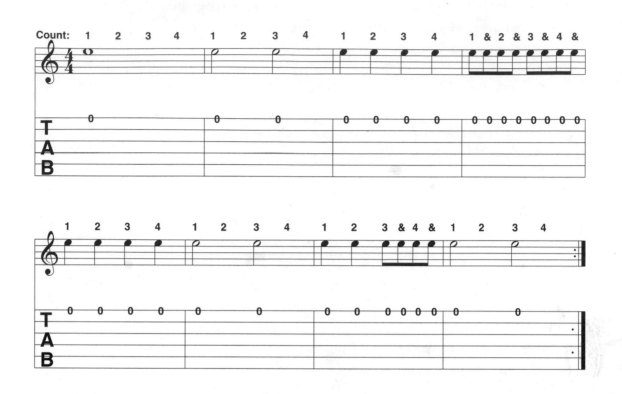

Left-Hand Fingering and Right-Hand Picking Technique

When playing single-note melodies (as in the following song, "Twinkle Twinkle Little Star") the general technique with the left-hand is to keep the fingers spread out one-finger-per-fret. If the 1st finger is being used at the 1st fret, the 2nd finger should be poised above the 2nd fret, the 3rd finger above the 3rd fret, and the 4th finger above the 4th fret.

With the right hand, play this tune with a pick using down-strokes only. (In Chapter 3 we will introduce upstrokes with the pick and in Chapter 6 we will see how to pluck single-note melodies with the right-hand fingers.)

Now, OK, we won't be bringing down the house at Carnegie Hall with this little ditty, no matter how rousing your rendition. But it's a start, right? Seriously, this puts into practice your knowledge of tablature, music reading, and technique with a relatively straightforward tune that enables you to hear for yourself whether you've got it right or not. So, play on!

Twinkle Twinkle Little Star
(Music by J. Green; Words by Jane Taylor)

Most of you will have gone straight to the tablature and will have used your knowledge of the tune to get the timing. That's fine; but once you've done that, go back and look at the note values and count along to it. Then look up the notes in the note dictionary on page 23 to confirm that you are playing the correct notes. There's a lot of information to put into practice here and a lot of technique points to be thinking of; just because this is a simple tune doesn't mean you should bash through it.

Notice the sharp between the treble clef and the time signature, on the F line. The arrangement of sharps or flats at the beginning of a piece of music is called a "key signature" and tells you what key you are in—we need not worry about this now. In practice, this particular key signature of F♯ means every time an F note is encountered (not just the F's on the top line) it must be played as F♯. However, in this particular song we do not encounter F.

Résumé

By now the principles behind reading music should be appreciated and understood. It literally takes years to become a good sight-reader on the guitar (sight reading is the ability to play a piece of music when it is seen for the first time). Remember, all the musical examples in this book are presented in music notation *and* tablature in order to help you find the notes on the guitar and the timing is kept as straightforward as possible.

Chapter **3**

Major and Seventh Chords

D and A7 Chords

In Chapter 1 we learned four easy chords—Easy G, Easy G7, Easy C, and Easy Gmaj7—meaning chords simplified from the form in which they are usually encountered. Now we will learn two "proper" chords—D and A7. A7 can be called simply A7 or A 7th. Strictly speaking, its full name would be A dominant 7th (we'll look at chord theory in Chapter 9).

Taking each of the chords in turn, play slowly through the chords from lowest string to highest string listening closely to each note produced. We want a clear note from each string. In order to do this, strings must be held down with the tips of the fingers: remember, the nails on the left hand must be kept very short. The three joints of the fingers should each be smoothly curved and the thumb should be roughly in the middle of the back of the neck, behind the 2nd finger (behind the 2nd fret for both the D and A7 chords).

Notice that the lowest note in the D chord, the open 4th string, is a D note and that the lowest note in the A7 chord is the open 5th string, which is an A note. This holds true for all the basic chords—the lowest note in a chord is the note the chord is "built from" (more on chord construction in Chapter 9) and this lowest note gives the chord its letter name. You can use this to remind you how many strings to play for a chord. For example, if, when fingering a D chord, you can't recall how many strings to play,

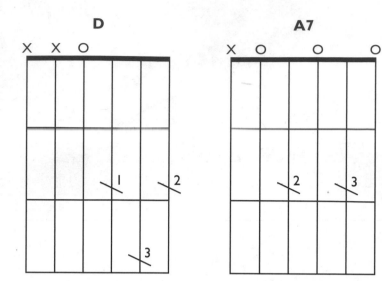

remember that the lowest note has to be a D note so the lowest note must be the 4th string, making a D chord a four-string chord.

Once the notes in the chords are sounding clearly, you can practice the change between D and A7. After strumming D once, lift fingers 1 and 2 from the strings, then relax the 3rd finger so it is no longer pressing the string against the fretboard, but is still in contact with the string. Then slide the 3rd finger down from the 3rd fret to the 2nd fret and press the string against the fretboard. It is now holding down the correct note for the A7 chord. Using a finger like this is called using it as a "guide" finger since it guides you into the next chord. Remember to relax the pressure before sliding the finger to the next note, otherwise you will produce an unwanted "sliding" sound, but don't relax the pressure so much that the finger lifts from the string, otherwise you won't be able to use it as a guide finger. Now place the 2nd finger on the 4th string 2nd fret and you are fingering the A7 chord.

The 3rd finger can also be used as a guide finger when changing from A7 to D. After strumming A7 once, lift the 2nd finger, slide the 3rd finger from the 2nd fret to the 3rd fret then place fingers 1 and 2 for the D chord. Once this technique of using the 3rd finger as a guide finger when changing between D and A7 has been absorbed, practice the following chord progression.

$\frac{4}{4}$ D///|A7///:||D

Remember, this means strum D four times, strum A7 four times, repeat from the beginning, then end with a single strum of the D chord. Practice slowly and tap your foot on the beat (four times to each bar). We are aiming to make the chord changes in time with the strumming and there is more chance of doing this if the exercise is played slowly.

The G Chord

There are three common fingerings of the G chord.

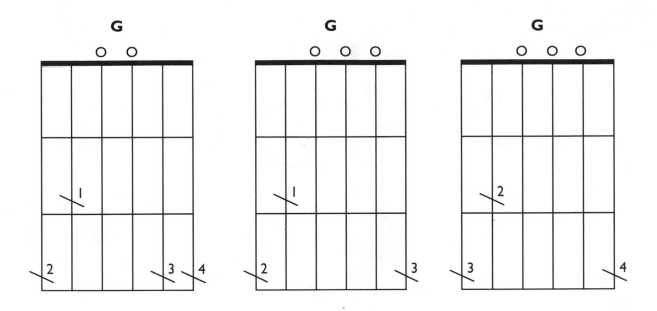

Note that the 2nd and 3rd versions contain exactly the same notes held down with different fingers, whereas the 1st version contains a different note altogether. In the 1st version the 2nd string is played at the 3rd fret, whereas the 2nd and 3rd versions contain the open 2nd string. Nevertheless, all three shapes are called G and, indeed, there are many other ways to play a G chord. Which version of G should be used depends on context—one version of G might be easier to get to from the chord that comes before. That is learned simply by experience. For now, we will use version 1 since it has a subtly "crisper" sound than versions 2 and 3 and also lends itself better to changing to and from D.

Before we tackle a chord progression joining together D, G, and A7, practice the change between D and G thus: finger the D chord and strum it once. Now lift fingers 1 and 2 but do not lift the 3rd finger—the 3rd finger stays on the same note for D and G chords. Then place fingers 1, 2, and 4 to form the G chord. This will take lots of practice before you can do it confidently and accurately! Strum the G chord once, then lift fingers 1, 2, and 4 and form the D chord. Again, this will require a lot of practice.

Once the change from D to G and from G to D is OK, strum through the following chord progression which uses D, A7, and G.

This is a common progression found in various forms in folk, country, and pop music. Take care in bar 7 where the D chord is strummed twice instead of four times, and is followed by the A7 chord, which is also strummed twice.

$$\frac{4}{4} \; D///|G///|D///|A7///|D///|G///|D/A7/|D///:||$$

Alternate Bass Pattern

All the chord progressions encountered so far have been played with downstrokes, strumming all the notes in each chord. The chord progression shown overleaf uses D, A7, and G and involves picking out a bass note (a note on strings 6, 5, or 4) then strumming the top three strings in the chord. For example, finger the D chord. Play the 4th string by itself then strum the top three strings of the D chord three times. Next, play the 5th string on its own (normally the 5th string doesn't belong with a D chord but it does in this case), strum the top three strings three times, then repeat from the beginning, starting with the open 4th string. Notice how the bass note, or lowest note, alternates between the 4th string and the 5th string, hence the term "alternate bass pattern." This type of accompaniment is found in country and folk music.

This is easiest to play when the progression is written out in music notation and tablature with the corresponding chord names. Notice how it says D for the first four bars (bar numbers are given above the treble clef at the beginning of each line): simply finger the D chord then all the notes you need are contained within the D chord. Again, use all downstrokes with the pick and play slowly. "Let notes ring" means just what it says—let the notes ring on until they die away naturally.

More Strumming Patterns

The alternate bass pattern discussed in the previous section provides variety to song accompaniments rather than just using downstrokes on the beat. Another way to make accompaniments more interesting is to introduce upstrokes with the pick. Signs are used to distinguish between different pick directions:

■ – a downstroke with the pick

V – an upstroke with the pick

Alternate Bass Pattern

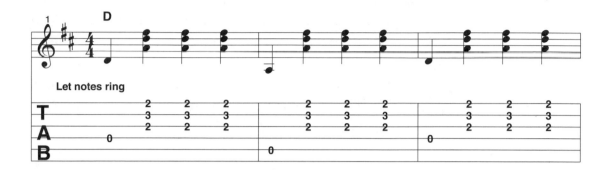

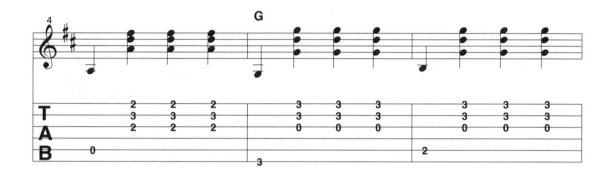

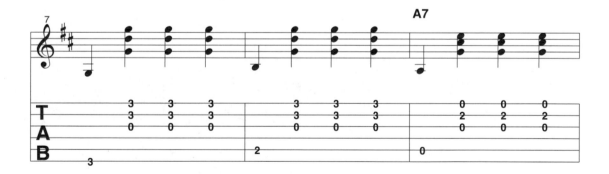

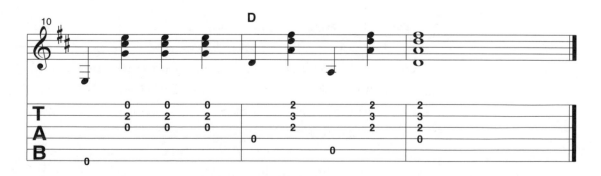

To get used to alternate strumming—strumming up and down continuously—finger the D chord then strum up and down, then repeat three more times. Don't hold the pick too hard and, with the up-strum, don't worry about hitting all four strings in the D chord, just concentrate on catching the top three strings. When playing an upstroke, the pick should lightly brush over the strings. Many beginners make the mistake of hitting the strings too hard, which interrupts a smooth, continuous strumming motion and risks getting the pick caught between the strings.

This rhythm and strumming pattern would be written in chord "slash" notation and looks like this. (The C time signature means "common time" which is $\frac{4}{4}$.)

The above pattern obviously lacks variety. The following variation is a suitable accompaniment pattern for many songs in $\frac{4}{4}$ time—the *crotchet*/eighth note strum on the first beat gives an emphasis to the first beat of the bar.

Use this strumming pattern to play the chord progression from the G Chord section earlier in this chapter.

$\frac{3}{4}$ Time Signature

So far in this book all the musical examples have been in $\frac{4}{4}$ time since this is the most common time signature. Another common time signature is $\frac{3}{4}$, in which there are three beats in the bar. $\frac{3}{4}$ is also known as "waltz time" since the dance known as the waltz has three beats in the bar.

The accompaniment from the Alternate Bass Pattern section can be adapted to $\frac{3}{4}$ time like this:

Alternate Bass Pattern in 3/4 Time

Similarly, the strumming pattern in 4/4 time can be adapted like this:

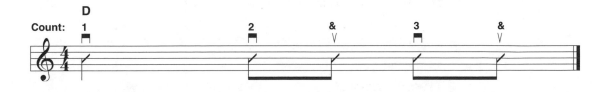

Practice Advice

Now that we have covered more musical material, it is worth stressing the importance of regular practice—it is more beneficial to practice for 20 minutes a day, at least five days a week than it is to practice for an hour on just two days a week.

Also, if a particular change is proving difficult, it is better to identify this problem and work on it in isolation. For example, when strumming the chord progression from the earlier G Chord section (page 31) if you find the change from D to G particularly difficult then practice this change over and over rather than playing through the whole progression several times. This way you are concentrating your efforts exactly where they are needed. Everyone progresses at different rates and it may take several days or even weeks before you feel confident and comfortable with certain chord changes, especially the changes that involve rearranging two, three, or even all four fingers of the left hand.

The D7 Chord

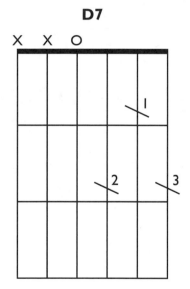

The D7 chord can be thought of as the "reversed shape" of the D chord.

Practice changing between D and D7 in the following progression: (Unfortunately, this change involves rearranging fingers 1, 2, and 3 with no scope for using a guide finger. Listen closely to the difference in sound between the two chords.)

$\frac{4}{4}$ D///|D///|D7///|D7///:||D

The D chord, being a major chord, sounds happy and positive. In contrast, the D7 chord sounds slightly tense and introduces an element of expectation—in musical terms, the D7 chord is "unresolved" and is resolved by changing to a G chord, as in the following progression. When executing the G to A7 change, use the 3rd finger as a guide finger—that is, don't lift it from the 2nd string but slide it down a fret leaving it on the correct note for A7.

$\frac{4}{4}$ D///|D///|D7///|D7///|G///|G///|A7///|A7///:||D

The E Chord

The E chord is commonly used by guitarists to check their tuning since it uses all six strings and contains three open strings.

As recommended earlier, whenever you learn a new chord you should play through it slowly, from lowest note to highest note, making sure all the notes sound clearly.

The E chord lends itself to a Spanish and flamenco-sounding chord progression when played with two related chord shapes that we will call F Spanish and G Spanish.

These two chords (shown opposite) may sound strange by themselves but in context with the E chord in the progression that follows they sound very effective and evocative. Notice that the F Spanish chord is the E chord shape with the fingers moved up a fret; similarly the G Spanish chord is the E chord shape with the fingers moved up three frets. Strictly speaking, F Spanish and G Spanish are not the chords' harmonically correct names (the correct names are rather complicated!) but these names will suffice for now since they contain half the notes from F and G chords respectively and are used in Spanish music.

When changing between these chords, as in the following progression, fingers 1, 2, and 3 can all be used as guide fingers to assist the chord changes: relax the fingers' pressure so that they are no longer holding down the note against the fretboard but leave the fingers in contact with the strings then slide the fingers to the next chord. Make sure you use the tips of the fingers to hold down notes and keep them as upright as possible in order not to touch the open strings in the chords. Since these are new chord shapes we will stick to downstrokes only with the pick, and since the example is in ⁴⁄₄ time there will be four downstrokes to the bar.

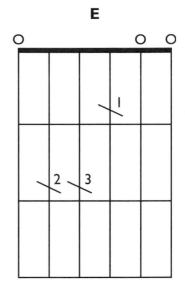

The E Chord

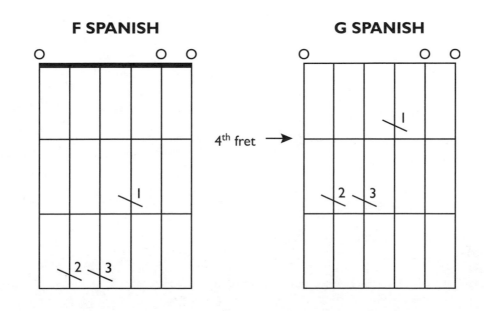

$\frac{4}{4}$ E///|F Spanish///|G Spanish///|F Spanish///:||E

Once you are comfortable with the above progression try this similar but harder progression that involves changing more quickly.

$\frac{4}{4}$ E///|F Spanish/G Spanish F Spanish:||E

Just to confirm you have interpreted the above progression correctly, it means strum E four times, strum F Spanish twice, G Spanish once, F Spanish once, then repeat from the beginning and end on a single strum of E.

Résumé

In this chapter we have learned the D, A7, G, and D7 chords. We have also learned the E chord, plus the F Spanish and G Spanish chords and have played these three chords in a couple of Spanish-flavored progressions. In terms of pick technique, we have learned alternate bass patterns in $\frac{4}{4}$ and $\frac{3}{4}$ and a strumming pattern in $\frac{4}{4}$ and $\frac{3}{4}$. We have also discussed how to practice most effectively.

To finish with, here is a chord progression that joins together all the main chords learned in this chapter:

$\frac{4}{4}$ D///|D///|D7///|D7///|G///|G///|E///|A7///:||D

Chapter **4**

Minor Chords and Ear Training

Dm Chord

The small "m" in a chord name is short for "minor," so the full name for Dm is D minor. Major chords do not have a similar means of notation; D is taken as being D major without any further notation specifically to denote major.

The Dm—D minor—chord is similar to the D chord, the difference being that in the D chord the top string is played at the 2nd fret, whereas in the Dm chord the top string is played at the 1st fret.

Here's a progression that uses Dm and A7. When you encounter new chords and new chord changes always look for common fingers between the chords or guide fingers that can be used to make changes easier. For example, in both Dm and A7 the 3rd finger is used on the 2nd string, so make sure you do not lift this finger when changing between these chords; instead, use it as a guide finger. In Chapter 3 we have already seen how the 3rd finger can be used as a guide finger when changing between D and A7, which assists the change (see page 30). The use of the 3rd finger as a guide finger also makes the following change easier:

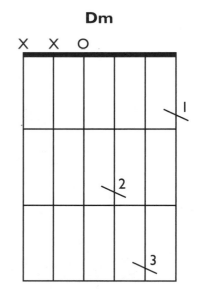

Dm

$\frac{4}{4}$ Dm///|A7///:||Dm

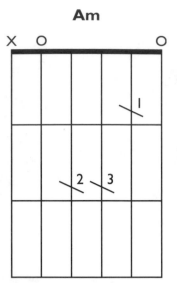

Am

Am Chord

Notice that the layout of the fingers for the Am chord is the same as for E, but the fingers are all placed a string higher.

Here's a chord progression that joins together Am, A7, and Dm. In both Am and A7 chords the 2nd finger is used on the 4th string 2nd fret. So make sure you do not lift the 2nd finger when making this change. Then, in the change from A7 to Dm, use the 3rd finger as a guide finger on the 2nd string (as in the previous section).

$\frac{4}{4}$ Am///IA7///IDm///IDm///:IIAm

Em and E7 Chords

Just as D was similar in shape to Dm, the previously learned E chord is similar in shape to Em and E7, as you can see from the chord diagrams opposite.

In the following chord progression, the first change is between Em and E7. Both chords use the 2nd finger on the 5th string 2nd fret, so make sure you do not lift the 2nd finger when changing between these chords. Unfortunately, there is no common finger between the next change in the progression—E7 to Am—so the fingers have to be lifted and replaced.

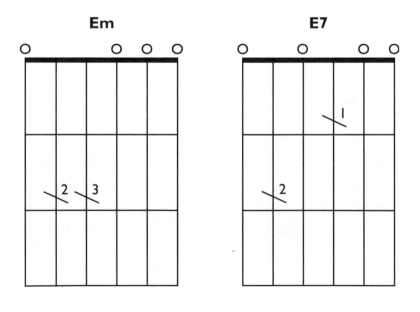

Em   **E7**

$\frac{4}{4}$ Em///IE7///IAm///IAm///:IIEm

Comparing the Sound of Major, Seventh, and Minor Chords

Learning a musical instrument not only involves the physical technique of moving your fingers in the appropriate manner, but also of developing your ear to hear, for example, the differences between different types of chord. The three main types of chord are major, seventh, and minor and at this stage you have learned D, D7, and Dm chords as well as E, E7, and Em chords. Now we will compare the different sounds and moods of these chords.

We have already learned that major chords have a happy and positive sound and 7 chords have a restless and "unresolved" sound; minor chords have a sad and unhappy sound. Now we will compare the sounds of these chords back-to-back in the following chord progression which involves strumming D once, letting it ring for four beats, strumming D7, letting it ring for four beats, then strumming Dm and letting it ring for four beats.

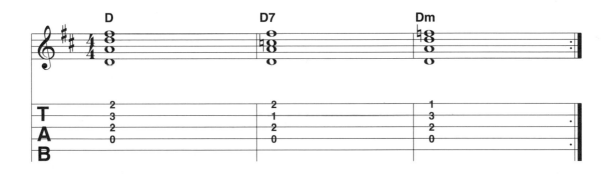

Listen closely to each of the chords. Listen for the differences—make sure you sound all the notes clearly, otherwise the chords may sound the same—then describe the sounds of the chords to yourself. Hearing different moods and feelings in chords and music is a subjective and personal thing, so two people may not hear the same chord in exactly the same way. Some people may think a major chord sounds "summery," or may think the minor chord sounds like the color black; the more you can identify features of a chord in a personal manner, the more you will be able to identify different types of chords.

After doing this exercise with D, D7, and Dm, do the same exercise with E, E7, and Em, thus:

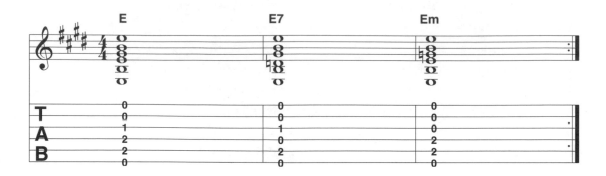

In musical terms we would describe this chord progression as being in a different key. Keys will be explored further in Chapter 9, but for now think of keys as "families" of chords that work together. For example, in Chapter 3 we saw how D, A7, and G work together—these chords are said to be in the key of D. When playing the two previous exercises you should be able to hear that the progression of major chord followed by 7 chord followed by minor chord has the same musical sound and effect regardless of whether you were playing the D, D7, and Dm or E, E7, and Em.

A useful exercise is to get a friend to play major, minor, or 7 chords to you and see if you can identify the type of chord correctly. You need not identify which specific chord it is, for example, whether it is a D chord or an E chord, because this is a quite separate, and considerably more advanced, skill. Alternatively, you could record yourself playing a series of chords mixing up D, D7, Dm, E, E7, and Em, making a note of the chords, then come back to it later and test yourself.

Comparing the Same Chord Progressions in Different Keys

In addition to being able to recognize chords as major, minor, or 7, another useful thing to be aware of is how the same chord progression can be played in different keys but keeps the same "overall sound." For example, in the Am Chord section we played the following chord progression, which was in the key of A minor:

$\frac{4}{4}$ Am/// |A7/// |Dm/// |Dm/// :||Am

Then in the Em Chord section we learned this chord progression, which is in the key of E minor:

$\frac{4}{4}$ Em///|E7///|Am///|Am///:||Em

Listen out for the similarity in "feel" between these two progressions; they are actually the same chord progressions but in different keys.

Bass Runs in $\frac{3}{4}$ Progression Using Am, Dm, Em, and E7

In Chapter 3 we looked at the alternate bass pattern for playing more interesting chord accompaniments (see page 33). The progression shown overleaf uses a similar alternate bass pattern but also has bass runs in bars 4, 8, and 12, which serve to link together the chords. "NC" in bars 4, 8, and 12 means "No Chord"—that is, there is no chord for these bars. Lift the fingers from the previous chord shape and play the single notes. The right-hand fingers to use for these notes are given beside the relevant note head in the music notation.

Résumé

In this chapter you have learned the Dm, Am, Em, and E7 chords, and learned to hear the difference between major, 7, and minor chords.

Bass Runs in 3/4 Progression

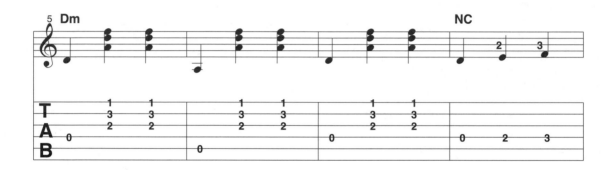

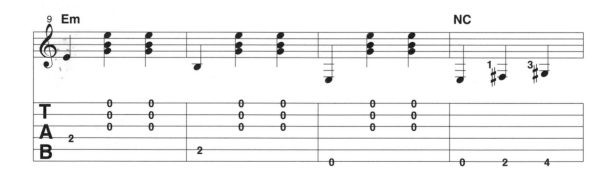

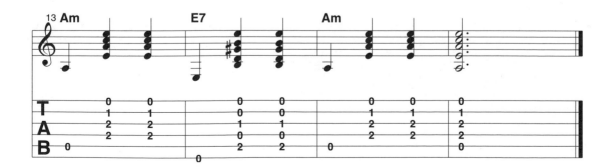

Chapter 5

The Twelve-Bar Blues

The Twelve-Bar Blues Progression

Most blues songs are based on a twelve-bar chord progression with set changes within the progression. Before we play a twelve-bar blues in E we need to learn a new chord: the B7 chord. Many beginners find B7 quite tricky since it involves all four fingers of the left hand.

To get used to fingering the B7 chord, play the following chord progression using E7 and B7. In both chords the 2nd finger is used on the 5th string 2nd fret, so make sure you do not lift this finger when changing between the chords.

B7

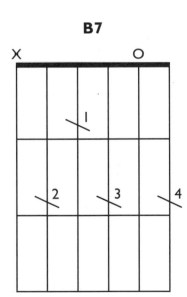

$\frac{4}{4}$ E7///|B7///:||E7

In the following twelve-bar blues, strum each chord once with a downstroke. Listen out for how the use of 7 chords gives the progression a feeling of forward momentum and restlessness.

$\frac{4}{4}$ E7///|A7///|E7///|E7///|
A7///|A7///|E7///|E7///|
B7///|A7///|E7///|B7///:||E7

Since this is such a common and standard chord progression, it ought to be memorized. For the sake of memorizing, this progression can be thought of in three sections, each section being four bars long.

While the twelve-bar blues is a set chord progression, some variations in the chord changes are possible, a common variation being to stay on E7 for the second bar. Another variation would be to stay on B7 for bar 10. Incorporating these two variations into the progression would make it:

$\frac{4}{4}$ E7///|E7///|E7///|E7///|
A7///|A7///|E7///|E7///|
B7///|B7///|E7///|B7///:||E7

Shuffle Blues in E

The two-chord progressions strummed in the previous section give the player the feel and sound of a twelve-bar blues, but as accompaniments they lack character—especially the second progression since it contains fewer changes than the first one. A more interesting and more common way to play a twelve-bar blues on the guitar is to use 5 and 6 chords, and the shuffle rhythm. Here are the E5 and E6 chords:

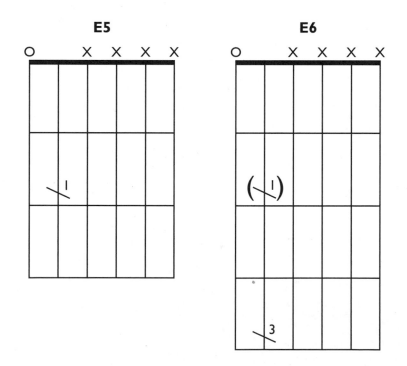

Since we are ultimately going to be changing back and forth between E5 and E6, when fingering the E6 chord leave the 1st finger on the 5th string 2nd fret, as indicated by the bracketed 1 in the E6 chord diagram. This doesn't make any difference to the sound of the chord but makes the chord change more efficient and reliable.

The numbers 5 and 6 in these chord names have nothing to do with the strings involved. The theory behind chord construction and naming will be looked at more closely in Chapter 9. For now, it is sufficient to know that the names arise from the fact that the E5 chord consists of an E note plus the fifth note from the E major scale. Similarly, the E6 chord consists of an E note plus the sixth note from the E major scale. This E5 shape is also known by rock guitarists as a "power chord" since it sounds effective when played with distortion, either from a distortion pedal or from an amplifier turned up near or at full volume. Playing, for example, the full six-string E chord with distortion would tend to sound messy and indistinct.

The shuffle rhythm is articulated when, instead of playing a chord or note in even *quavers*, the first *quaver* on each beat is held onto for slightly longer and the second *quaver* is shortened. This gives the rhythm a lilting or "bouncy" feel and sounds like "duuh-da, duuh-da, duuh-da, duuh-da." If a song is to be played in the shuffle rhythm it will say "Shuffle," "Shuffle feel," "Triplet feel," "Swing," or have the following sign at the beginning:

In Shuffle Blues in E on page 49 the names of the chords are given above the music notation. As you can see, the entire progression uses 5 and 6 chords, consisting of only two notes. Technique wise, remember to keep the fingers spread out one-finger-per-fret with the left hand, with the thumb behind the 2nd finger and in the middle of the neck at the back—not too high, not too low. A5 and A6 are simply the E5 and E6 chord shapes played on strings 5 and 4, as will be seen from the tablature. To complete the blues in this style we also need B5 and B6 chords.

These are movable chord shapes; they don't use any open strings so they can be moved up or down the fretboard. These chords take their letter names from the lower of the two notes in the chord, which is B. If the B5 chord shape is moved up one fret (the left hand is moved towards your right hand) the chord

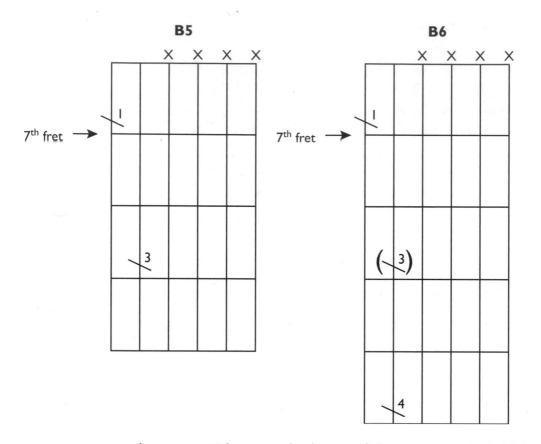

becomes C5 because the lower of the two notes is C. This movable shape will be used in Shuffle Blues in E II (see page 51).

Since we are going to be changing between the B5 and B6 chords you can leave the 3rd finger in place from B5 when changing to B6. It doesn't make any difference to the sound, but makes the chord change easier. B6, as you will no doubt feel, is a bit of a stretch, and may take a few days or even weeks of practice before you feel comfortable with it. By now you should have calluses on the ends of your fingers; playing the guitar also requires independence between the fingers and the ability to stretch. To facilitate this particular stretch for B6, move the left-hand thumb slightly closer to the ground and push the left-hand wrist forward slightly—this enables the fingers to stretch further.

In the change at the end of bar 8 into bar 9, from E6 to B5, leave the 3rd finger in contact with the 5th string and slide it up the string. Using the 3rd finger as a guide finger makes this change easier. With the right hand, use all downstrokes with the pick—this is the easiest way to hit two strings repeatedly with accuracy, and will produce a consistent tone (there is a subtle difference in tone between downstrokes and upstrokes).

Shuffle Blues in 'E'

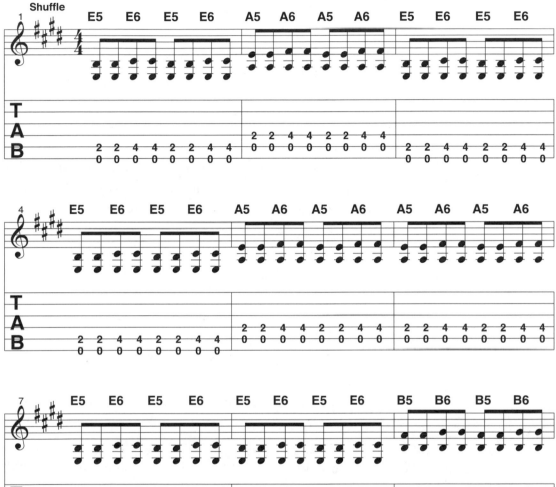
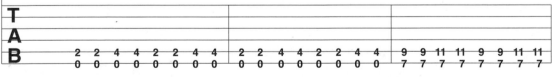
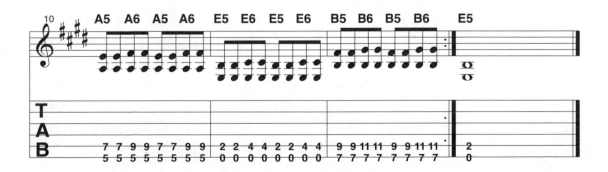

The progression in bar 1 is a common blues riff. "Riff" is a term used in blues, rock, country, and jazz, a riff being a short series of chords or single notes that is often played at the beginning of the song and repeated at other points in the song. Examples of songs that include famous opening riffs include Deep Purple's "Smoke on the Water," Jimi Hendrix's "Purple Haze" (which actually includes three different riffs in the introduction), and Nirvana's "Smells Like Teen Spirit."

Notice how, in Shuffle Blues in E (page 49), there are two different fingerings for A5 and A6. In bars 2, 5, and 6 these chords are played low down the fretboard on strings 5 and 4; in bar 10 these chords are played higher up the fretboard on strings 6 and 5. Compare the sounds of the chords: you will be able to hear that they are the same pitch, but that there is a slight difference in tone—the chords on the bottom two strings have a slightly darker, bassier tone because they are played on thicker strings and higher up the fretboard. The reason A5 and A6 are played on the bottom two strings in bar 10 is that they are easier to get to from the previous bar of B5 and B6.

Once you are confident with this you can get an interesting effect by playing with "palm muting." This involves resting the palm of the right hand on the strings close to the bridge. This produces a "chunky" sound. Initially, place the palm very close to the bridge for a light muting effect. If the hand is too far from the bridge, the strings will be too dampened to produce a musical sound. Once you have the hang of the technique, experiment with how changing the distance between the palm and the bridge produces different effects.

Shuffle Blues in E II

Now we are going to add two runs to Shuffle Blues in E using the movable 5 chord shape. The first run is in bar 4. Notice how playing the B5 shape at frets 2 and 4 produces an F#5 chord since the name of the note at the bottom of the chord (bottom string second fret) is F#. It is the same for the following G5 and G#5 chords—the lower note in these two chords is G and G#, respectively. Notice how, after the initial jump from E5 to F#5, the chords in this run move up one fret at a time. This is known as a "chromatic" progression, that is, one in which the notes move in consecutive frets.

Shuffle Blues in 'E' II

The other run is in bar 11 and is also based on the movable 5 chord. Again, after the initial jump from E5 to G♯5, the chords move chromatically. Play the whole progression slowly. It will probably be necessary to take out the two new bits (bars 4/5 and bars 11/12) and practice them in isolation, over and over, until the changes are smooth.

Shuffle Variations

To create a more interesting blues progression we will add an E7 chord to the first bar. Remember how you learned that chords can be fingered in different ways? (Chapter 3, page 31.) Well, you learned the open E7 chord in Chapter 4 (page 40) but this E7 is a reduced version, consisting of only two notes to fit in with the E5 and E6 chords. This time you can work out the chord from the tablature rather than a chord diagram and you should be able to deduce for yourself that this chord should be played with the 4th finger since it follows on from the E5 and E6 chords.

Bar 9 involves what may seem at first to be a pretty horrendous stretch to reach the B7 chord (again, it's not the B7 chord we learned at the beginning of this chapter!). Remember: to stretch further, move the left-hand thumb slightly closer to the ground and push the wrist slightly forward. This bar will almost certainly require isolated practice. If you haven't stretched your fingers before, you will surprise yourself as to what you can achieve but don't overdo it—if it hurts, stop, then try again after the discomfort has gone. Practice this bar for three minutes every day for a week and you will make significant progress.

Bars 11 and 12 use a common blues "turnaround." A turnaround is a progression found in bars 11 and 12 of a twelve-bar blues that leads the accompaniment back into the main progression. For the E7 chord in bar 11 (yet again, it's not the E7 we learned in Chapter 4) use fingers 3 and 2—3rd finger on the 3rd string 4th fret and 2nd finger on the 2nd string 3rd fret. Slide both fingers down a fret to produce the A♯dim chord (sounds complicated—but it's not), slide both fingers down again to finger the Am chord, then slide the 3rd finger down again to produce the E chord—the 2nd finger is not needed for this chord. Then, slide the 3rd finger up three frets so it's in place for the new chord in bar 12: the C7 chord.

C7

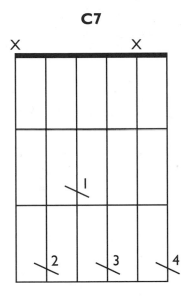

This C7 is not the most common form of the chord (we will look at C7 in Chapter 7) but fits in very nicely with this turnaround. Notice that this version of C7 is the B7 chord shape moved one fret higher. The "x" above the 2nd string means this string is not to be played, but the strings on either side have to be played. This is done by damping the 2nd string by lightly touching it with the side of the 3rd finger—the 3rd finger has to be held slightly flatter than normal in order to achieve this. This results in a dull "thonk" when the 2nd string is struck which is lost among the other notes in the C7 chord when the full chord is struck.

Notice that above the very last two bars there's a 1 plus a bracket and a 2 plus a bracket. This means that the first time you play through the progression you play the bar with 1 above it; you then repeat from the beginning and at the end of the second time you play the bar with 2 above it. The curved lines in these two bars are called "ties." Ties join together notes of the same pitch, so hit the notes once and give them the combined note length.

But enough of my yakkin'—let's play!

Shuffle Variations

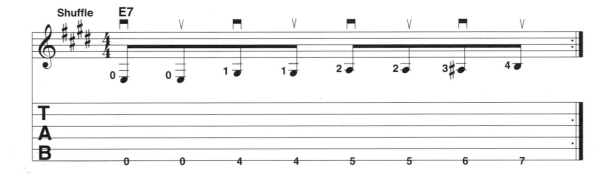

Jazz/Blues Bass Riff

This has been called the Jazz/Blues Bass Riff for the simple reason
that it is a riff commonly played in jazz and blues and is played on
the bass guitar or the double bass or on the bass strings (the bottom three strings) of the guitar. Instead of following the twelve-bar
blues progression with chords, as we did with Shuffle Blues in E,
Shuffle Blues in E II, and Shuffle Variations, we'll now follow the
twelve-bar blues in E with this single-note riff. Here's the riff in E7
(this riff would go along with an E7 chord). The left-hand fingers
to use are indicated beside the notes in the music.

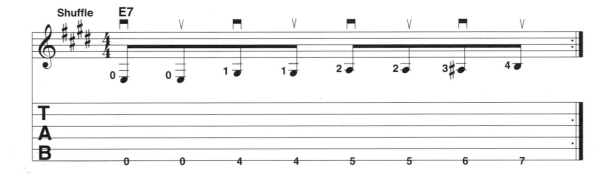

Apart from being fun to play (hopefully!), this riff serves two
useful technique purposes. First, as seen from the pick directions
above the notes in the music, it is marked to be played with alternate picking, that is, down-up-down-up, etc. Also, as you can see
from the left-hand finger indications, this riff uses all four fingers
of the left hand and provides an excellent opportunity to work on
left-hand finger technique. Even before starting, the fingers should
be spread out one-finger-per-fret, poised above the frets to be
played, with the thumb behind the 2nd finger. As you progress
through the riff, leave the fingers down so when you get to the
end of the riff all four fingers are on the fretboard.

To follow the complete twelve-bar blues with this riff, the
sequence of notes has to be played for an A7 chord (which is
simply the E7 riff starting on the open A string) and for a B7
chord (which requires some re-fingering as shown in bar 9 of the
following progression). "Sim" means "simile"; that is, continue in
a similar manner.

Jazz/Blues Bass Riff

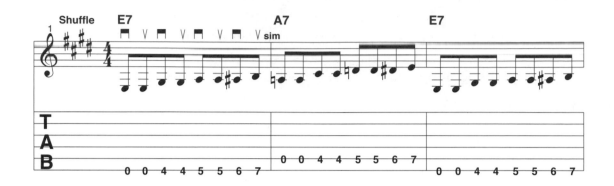

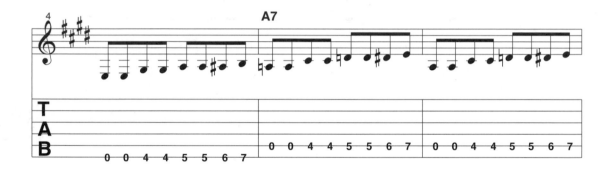

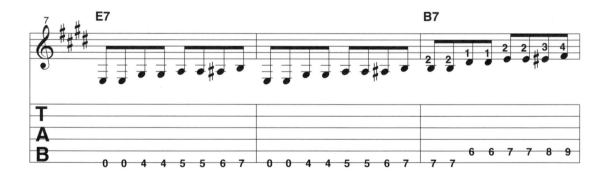

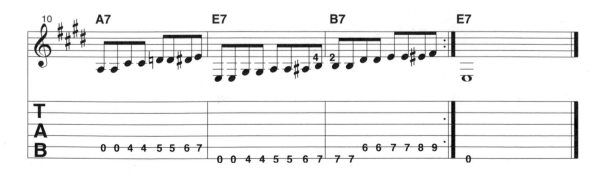

Slightly more difficult than the Jazz/Blues Bass Riff, this riff is common in blues and rock 'n' roll and is, again, played with alternate picking. It's slightly harder than the Jazz/Blues Bass Riff because the E7 and A7 versions of the riff are played on two strings, and the B7 version of the riff involves three strings. Here's the E7 version of the riff; in preparation for this riff, place the 1st finger on the 5th string 2nd fret and leave it there.

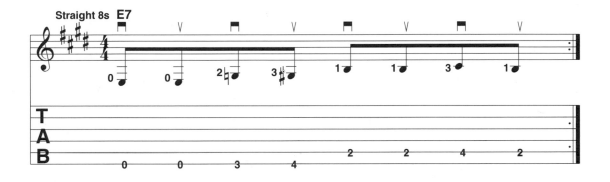

As you will see from the lack of a shuffle direction, this riff is not played in the shuffle rhythm. When the *quavers*/eighth notes are given equal value the rhythm is called "straight 8s." Normally there is no need to say this since it is automatically assumed if there is no shuffle direction.

On the following page, is the Boogie riff in a twelve-bar progression. Care must be taken with the B7 riff since it is played over three strings at the bottom of the fretboard, therefore the fingers must be kept spread out one-finger-per-fret where the gaps between the frets are largest.

Boogie Variations Riff

This takes the Boogie riff and makes it two bars long by adding an "answering" phrase after the original Boogie riff. Here's the E7 version of the riff:

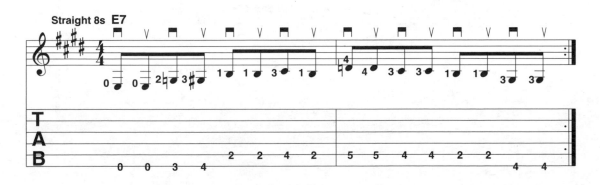

Boogie Riff

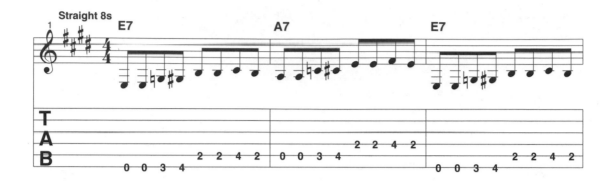

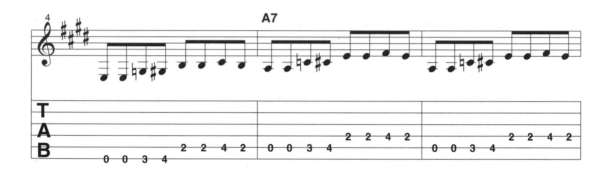

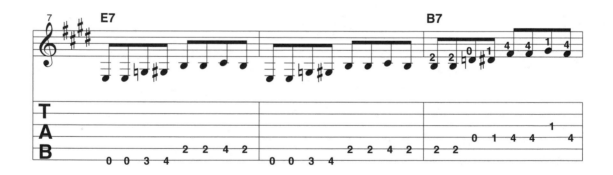

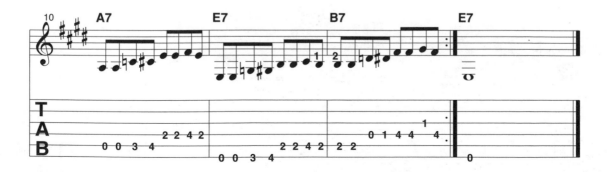

Boogie Variations

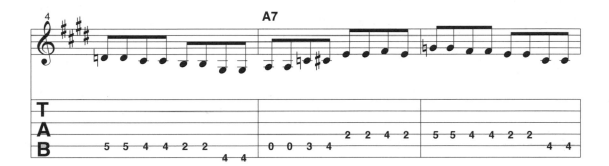

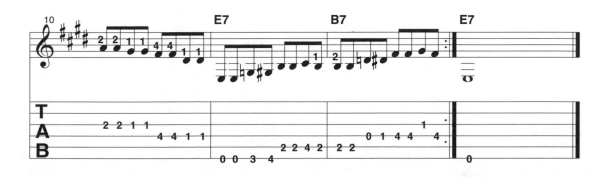

Yet again, the riff is played with alternate picking. Since the basic riff is now two bars long we will use the second version of the twelve-bar blues from the first section of this chapter—this stays on the B7 chord for two bars in bars 9 and 10, thus enabling the full version of the riff to be played for a B7 chord. Bars 11 and 12 are one bar each on E7 and B7, so only the first bar of the riff is played.

Résumé

You should be able to play five versions of a twelve-bar blues in E, two strumming full open chords, and three playing two-note chord riffs. Your alternate picking technique has been refined by playing the Jazz/Blues Bass Riff, Boogie Riff, and Boogie Variations Riff in twelve-bar blues progressions. You should know what is meant by riff, shuffle, power chord, palm muting, turnaround, and straight 8s.

Chapter 6

Classical Guitar

Posture

As stated in Chapter 1, classical guitar has a prescribed way of sitting, intended to maximize the player's potential by enabling the hands to work in the most efficient and effective manner. A footstool is used for the left foot in order to heighten the guitar and bring it into a more favorable position for playing. If you don't have a footstool, a pile of books will suffice in the meantime; in the longer term, an adjustable footstool would be better. (Having said that, some classical players find that prolonged use of a footstool can induce back strains!) There are alternatives to the footstool, such as placing a cushion on the left thigh to raise the height of the guitar. A shop specializing in classical guitars will be able to advise.

Sit at the front of a medium-height stool or chair with no arms. The left leg should be at right angles to the body and point forwards, with the left foot elevated by a footstool. The hollow of the guitar rests on the top of the left thigh, so the back of the guitar touches the chest, with the neck of the guitar sloping gently upwards. The right leg is angled away from the guitar and the base of the guitar rests on the right inner thigh. With the right forearm resting lightly on the top of the guitar, the guitar should be securely held in place by these four points of contact—top of the right leg thigh, bottom of the chest, inner left thigh, and right forearm on the top of the guitar.

Correct Posture for Classical Guitar Playing

We have already discussed the correct position and technique of the left-hand. This is even more important in classical playing which can place greater demands on the left hand. To re-cap, the main points are:

1) the fingers should be spread out one-finger-per-fret with the thumb behind the 2nd finger and in the middle of the neck;

2) notes should be held down by the tips of the fingers (so, nails must be kept short) and the fingers should be smoothly curved throughout each of the three finger joints;

3) only the thumb and the fingertips touch the guitar.

In classical guitar playing, the fingers of the right hand are used to pluck the strings. The best tone is produced by plucking

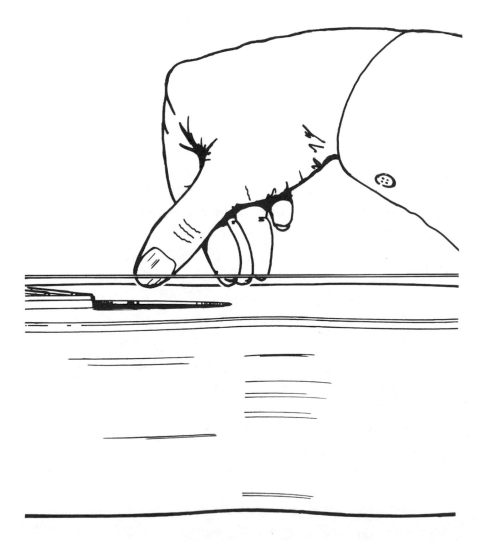

Right Hand Positioning

the strings with a combination of flesh and nail, so the nails should extend slightly over the edge of the fingertips. If the nails are too long, the sound will be too trebly and plucking will be difficult to control; if the nails are too short and the string is plucked with flesh only, the sound will be quiet and lack definition.

With the right forearm lightly resting on the top of the guitar, the wrist slightly curved to bring the right hand above the strings, which part of the forearm rests on the top of the guitar depends on the length of one's arms and will require some experimentation. The line of the knuckles should be parallel to the strings and roughly above the 3rd string.

The general position of the fingers is that the index, middle, and ring fingers should gently slope to the right as you look down on them (this means the strings are plucked with the left-hand side of the fingers) and the thumb should slope to the left. The intersection of the thumb and index finger forms an "x" shape.

The right hand should be placed at the right-hand side of the sound hole as you look down—if the hand is over the sound hole it blocks the sound coming out of the sound hole, resulting in a muffled tone and reduced volume.

Obviously, there are many things to bear in mind here, and one aspect of technique can affect another.

Rest Strokes and Free Strokes

There are different techniques for plucking strings—rest strokes or *apoyando* (to give them their Spanish name), and free strokes or *tirando*. A rest stroke is when the plucking finger or thumb moves through a string then comes to rest on the next string. A free stroke is when the plucking finger or thumb moves through a string then moves over the top of the next string.

There is a difference in tone and volume between rest and free strokes—a rest stroke produces a louder and fuller tone, so it tends to be used for single-note melodies or for bringing a melody out above an accompaniment, whereas free strokes tend to be used for *arpeggio* accompaniments.

Practice rest and free strokes on the open top string. Play the string, for example, eight times, alternating middle and index fingers with rest strokes, then do the same again with free strokes.

Technique Exercises

Here are three technique exercises to put the above techniques into practice. The first two exercises are primarily for the left-hand fingers, although you should obviously strive to keep the right hand in the correct position. Right-hand notation for classical guitar is derived from the Spanish words for the fingers. Hence, the thumb is *pulgar,* shortened to "p," the index finger is *indice,* shortened to "i," the middle finger is *medio,* shortened to "m," and the ring finger is *annular,* shortened to "a."

This first exercise is played solely on the top string. Remember: even before you start playing, the fingers should be spread out one-finger-per-fret, thumb behind the 2nd finger, fingers poised close above the frets on which they are going to be used. The fingers should be smoothly curved throughout each of the three finger joints. As explained previously, "sim" is short for "simile," which means "in a similar manner" and in this case means alternate middle and index fingers to pluck the notes. Play the exercise several times with rest strokes, then several times with free strokes. When playing on the top strings with the fingers and not using the thumb of the right hand, it is perfectly acceptable to rest the thumb lightly on the bottom string, thereby giving the hand greater stability.

This second exercise is the same pattern of notes as the previous exercise, but played on the bottom string. In order to reach the bottom string more comfortably, the left-hand thumb should be moved slightly closer to the ground, thereby enabling the left wrist to be pushed forward. The fingers should remain curved but should be slightly less curved than when playing on the top string. Again, practice this slowly, with rest and free strokes with the thumb. When playing on the bottom string with the thumb and not using the fingers, it is perfectly acceptable to rest the three fingers on the top three strings—index on 3rd, middle on 2nd, ring finger on 1st—in order to achieve greater stability.

The third technique exercise is for the right hand only and involves an open string *arpeggio*. An *arpeggio* is when the notes of a chord are played one at a time; in this case the open strings from the Em chord. *Arpeggios* are usually played with free strokes so there's no need to practice this exercise with rest strokes. Make sure you can see the "x" shape between the right-hand thumb and index finger.

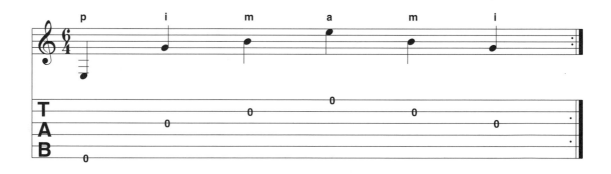

"Asturias" by Albéniz

Originally written by the Spanish composer Isaac Albéniz (1860–1909) for piano, "Asturias" was transcribed for the classical guitar and has become part of the standard classical guitar repertoire. Rest assured, the version you will play in the exercise on page 69 is a simplified and shortened version of what you would hear in concert!

This piece introduces *semiquavers* (or sixteenth notes), which in the time signature of $\frac{4}{4}$ (4 beats in the bar with each beat being a *crotchet*) are worth a quarter of a beat. *Semiquavers* look similar to *quavers* except they have two "tails" coming from the note stem. To count them, the beat is subdivided into 4 (represented by "1, e, &, a," and so forth to help), as in the following exercise with *semiquavers*.

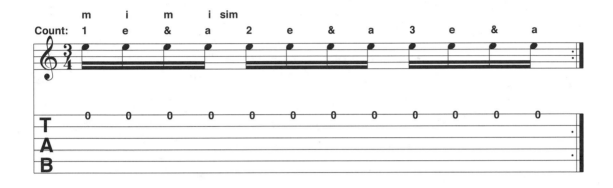

Here's a counting exercise mixing *crotchets, quavers,* and *semi-quavers.* Remember to count aloud and tap your foot on the beat, not to the note rhythm.

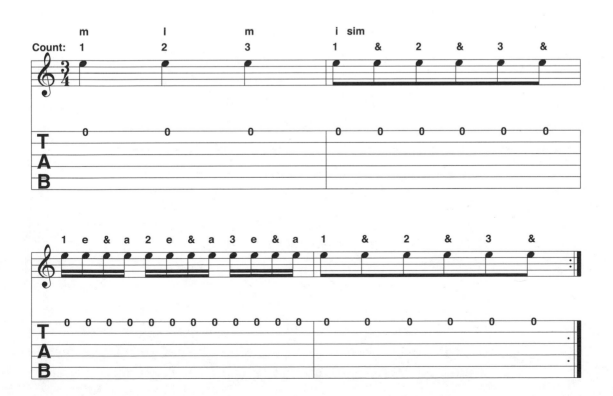

Before we tackle "Asturias" we will isolate the physical techniques required of each hand to play it. First, we will look at the right-hand movements required to play this tune, but using solely open strings. This will enable us to concentrate on the correct hand position. Classical guitar music usually has two or even more parts—that is, there is a melody *and* an accompaniment being played at the same time. In "Asturias" a melody is played on the bass strings and the open top string is played after each melody note, providing a very simple accompaniment. Let the top string ring on—do not put the middle finger back onto the string. Playing with free strokes, this technique can be practiced thus:

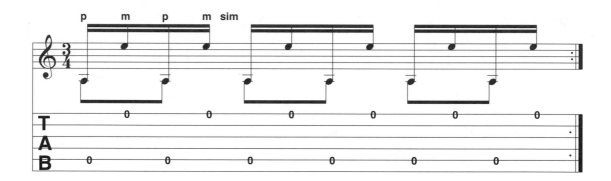

As already stated, the melody in this tune is played on bass strings, so we will look at the opening bar of the melody. The left-hand technique is to keep the fingers spread out one-finger-per-fret.

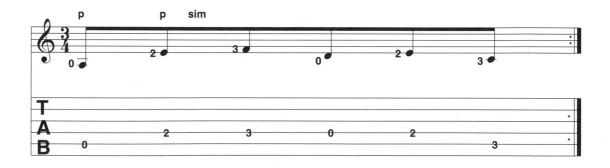

Now that we have practiced the right- and left-hand techniques we are ready to tackle the tune. Do not be put off by the length of the tune—there's quite a lot of repetition. Tackle a bar at a time,

Asturias by Albéniz
(arranged by Douglas J. Noble)

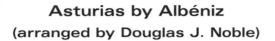

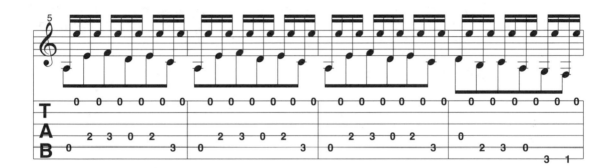

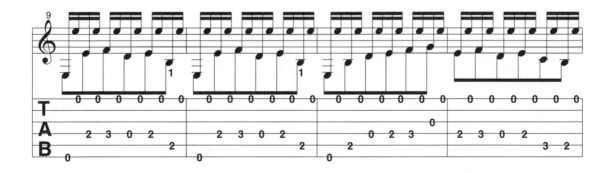

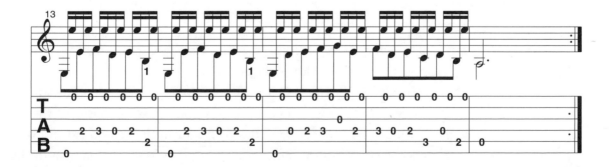

then piece together each line in turn rather than trying to tackle the whole tune in one go. In bars 9 and 13 we have to deviate from the one-finger-per-fret fingering. This is because there are two consecutive bass notes at the 2nd fret and a general rule of left-hand fingering is that the same finger should not be used for two notes in a row on different strings since there is bound to be an audible gap between the notes as the finger moves from one string to another. The fingering to be used is indicated beside the notes in the music. Make sure you hold on to the bass note while plucking the upper note, otherwise the bass melody will sound disjointed and *staccato*.

"Malagueña" (traditional)

"Malagueña" is a traditional form of the fandango dance from the Málaga region of Spain. As with "Asturias," before we tackle this piece we will practice the right- and left-hand techniques and the picking technique required to play it using solely open strings—this will enable us to concentrate on the correct hand position.

The right-hand technique is similar to that in "Asturias," but this time the accompaniment is on the top two strings instead of just the open top string. So, the index finger plucks the 2nd string and the middle finger plucks the top string thus:

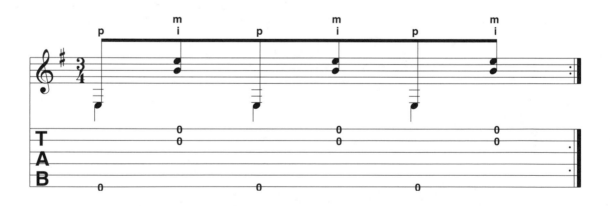

The left-hand technique is again one-finger-per-fret, but this time it involves position shifting—that is, the one-finger-per-fret pattern has to be shifted to start at a different fret, making sure you move the thumb when you move the fingers. Practice the first line of the melody below with the fingering indicated on the music notation—the position shift is at the end of the 2nd bar, going into the 3rd bar.

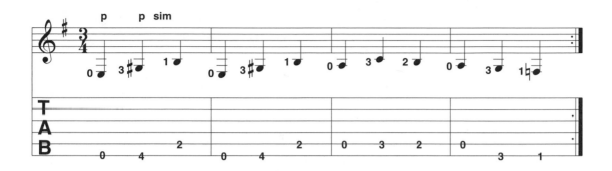

Now we are ready to tackle the tune. Care must be taken in bars 3 and 4—the accompaniment involves playing the 2nd string at the 1st fret with the 1st finger. Make sure the 1st finger is kept upright so that it doesn't touch the top string. The end of the 4th bar involves a slightly awkward stretch whereby the 1st finger remains on the 2nd string 1st fret while the 2nd finger reaches to the bottom string 1st fret. Again, practice a bar at a time, then a line at a time.

Résumé

You have learned the main points of classical guitar technique. Obviously, there are a lot of points to get right at the same time and if one aspect isn't quite correct it can affect all the others. The two key words here are patience and perseverance. You cannot learn classical guitar in the same way as you learned the Easy chords in Chapter 1—it's an altogether more sophisticated and refined skill. You have learned two classical tunes, "Asturias" and "Malagueña."

Malagueña

(Traditional, arranged by Douglas J. Noble)

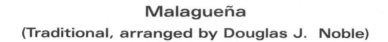

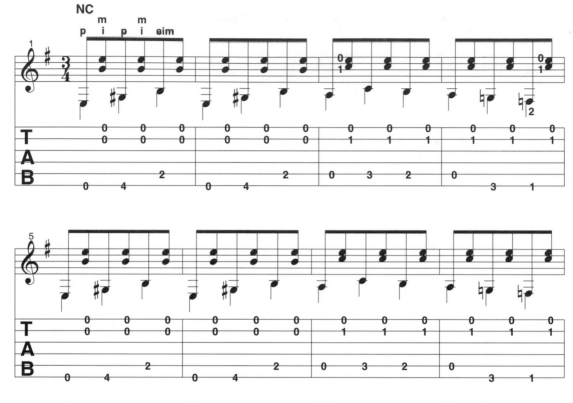

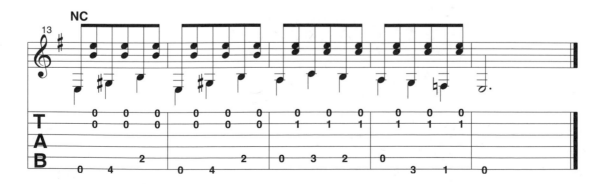

Chapter 7

Completing the Open String Chords

The A Chord

Here are two ways of fingering the A chord: the traditional fingering on the left, with the alternative fingering on the right. Try both. Those with large fingers and those playing on an acoustic guitar may find the alternative second fingering easier.

Here's a progression involving A, D and E. Whichever fingering for A you are using, the 3rd finger can be used as a guide finger on the 2nd string when changing from A to D and from D to A. If you are using the alternative second fingering for A, the 1st finger can be used as a guide finger when changing from A to E and from E to A. This is another standard chord progression heard in many songs, including Buddy Holly's "Peggy Sue."

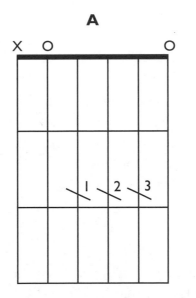

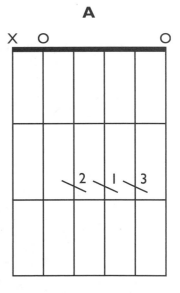

$\frac{4}{4}$ A///|D///|A///|E///|A///|D///|A/E/:||A

The C, C7, and F Chords

Generally speaking, F is the most difficult of all the basic open chords. Technically it isn't really an open chord since it doesn't use any open strings, but it's a very useful chord to include here since it enables chord progressions to be played in the common key of C, the main chords of which are C, Am, F, and G.

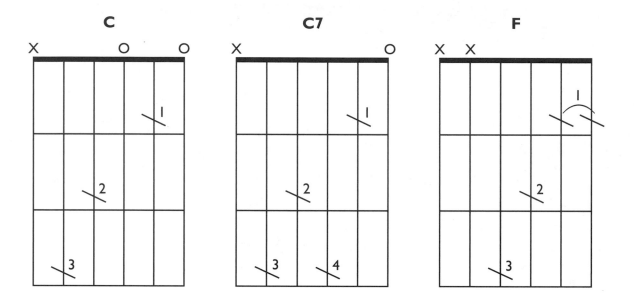

F is a tricky chord because it involves a "partial *barré*." A *barré* is when a finger, normally the 1st finger, is used to hold down two or more notes at the same fret on different strings. A "full *barré*" is when the 1st finger holds down all six strings; a "partial *barré*" is when the 1st finger holds down anywhere from two to five strings. (*Barrés* will be looked at in more depth in Chapter 8.)

For this F chord, the 1st finger holds down strings 1 and 2 at the 1st fret. Unlike when playing on one string at a time, the tip of the 1st finger has to be laid flat across the fretboard, running parallel to the fret. Don't use more of the finger than necessary, so the 1st finger should not touch the 3rd string.

The change from C to C7 is straightforward—all you need do is add the 4th finger to the 3rd string 3rd fret. Here's a progression with C, C7, and F:

$\frac{4}{4}$ C///|C7///|F///|F///:||C

G7 Chord

The G7 chord is the one remaining chord from the fifteen basic open chord shapes. G7 is often preceded by G and thus it will be seen that the change from G to G7 is easier if the third of the three fingerings for G from Chapter 3's G Chord section is used—this alternative fingering is repeated here.

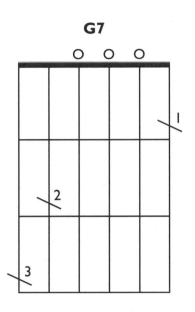

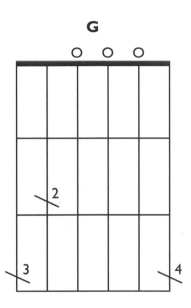

Here's a common chord progression involving G, G7, and C. Practice using both the four-finger version of G and the alternative fingering above. Notice how, when using the alternative fingering of G changing to G7, only the note on the top string has to be changed.

Now here's a common chord progression involving C and G7. Notice how the G7 shape is similar to the C shape but "widened," as it were.

$\frac{4}{4}$ C///|C///|G7///|G7///:||C

Three Standard Chord Progressions

Certain chord progressions are repeated in various songs in slightly different guises. Here's a progression that can be heard in the '50s pop songs "Unchained Melody" and "Stand By Me" and revisited and updated by Sting in the '80s for the Police's "Every Breath You Take."

$\frac{4}{4}$ C///|Am///|F///|G///:||C

This chord progression can be made more interesting by *arpeggiating* the chords—that is, playing through the notes in the chord one at a time, in triplets. "Triplets" are when there are three notes to a beat and they are written as three *quavers* joined or

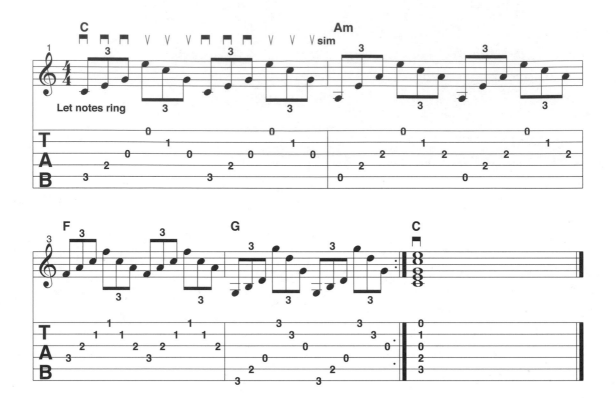

beamed together with a "3" above or below the beam. The counting for each bar of the above exercise is "ONE-two-three-TWO-two-three-THREE-two-three-FOUR-two-three." Notice the pick directions.

Here's the same progression in the key of G: strum through this progression then *arpeggiate* it in the same way you have just played the previous chord progression.

$\frac{4}{4}$ G///|Em///|C///|D///:||G

Now here's a second standard chord progression which can be heard (in various forms) in many rock songs including Led Zeppelin's "Stairway to Heaven," Bob Dylan's "All Along the Watchtower" (also famously covered by Jimi Hendrix), and Oasis's "Stand By Me" (not the Ben E. King song!).

$\frac{4}{4}$ Am///|G///|F///|G///:||Am

Below is the strumming pattern from the More Strumming Patterns section of Chapter 3 (page 32) applied to this chord progression. Note that the rhythmic value of the final strum is a *semibreve*.

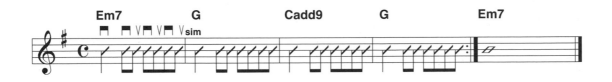

Here's the same progression in the key of E minor.

$\frac{4}{4}$ Em///|D///|C///|D///:||Em

Once you can change between the chords smoothly, strum it in the rhythm used to treat the previous chord progression.

Now here's a third common chord progression that you should work on in the same way:

$\frac{4}{4}$ A///|A7///|D///|Dm///|A///|E7///|A///|A///:||

"House Of The Rising Sun"

A perennial favorite of guitarists everywhere, the traditional "House of the Rising Sun" was made famous by the Animals' version, which reached the top of the British singles charts in 1964. Here's the chord progression for the song.

$\frac{4}{4}$ Am//|C//|D//|F//|Am//|C//|E//|E//|
Am//|C//|D//|F//|Am//|E//|Am//|Am//||

Next, here's the melody of the song, played on the bass strings with the corresponding words. Notice this melody doesn't begin on the first beat of the bar—it begins on the third beat of the bar. Since the first bar only contains one beat, the last bar has to contain two beats so that the first and last bars add up to a complete bar.

House of the Rising Sun (Melody)

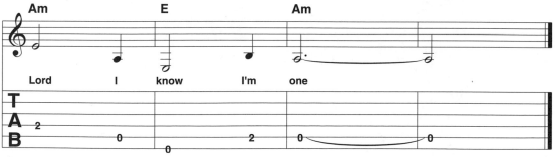

Now, in the following fingerpicking arrangement of "House of the Rising Sun" we are able to combine the melody plus an *arpeggio* accompaniment. In order to accommodate the melody into the chords a variation is needed on the F chord—we need to play an F/C chord. This "slash chord" notation means an F chord but with a C note at the bottom of it—in Chapter 3's D and A7 Chords section (page 29) we saw how the lowest note of a chord is normally the same as the letter name of the chord. For example, in the standard F chord, the lowest note—check this for yourself!—is an F note. The lowest note in F/C—again, check this out for yourself!—is a C note.

Next we will look at the fingerpicking pattern used for this arrangement. Finger the Am chord shape, and you will be already holding down all the notes you need.

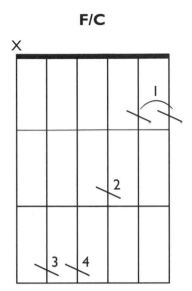

F/C

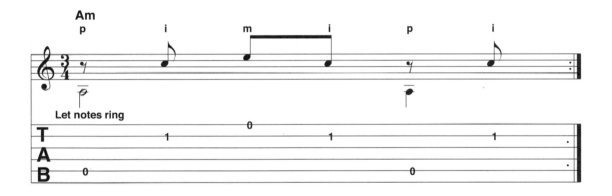

Now we are ready to play the complete arrangement. Remember, the melody is on the bass strings and is indicated by the notes with stems that point downwards, so make sure these notes are clearly audible and louder than the accompaniment. The fingerpicking pattern is altered slightly in bars 7, 15, and 16, in order to accommodate the melody.

House of the Rising Sun

(Traditional, arranged by Douglas J. Noble)

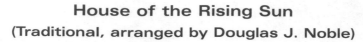

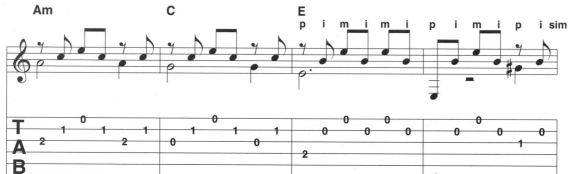

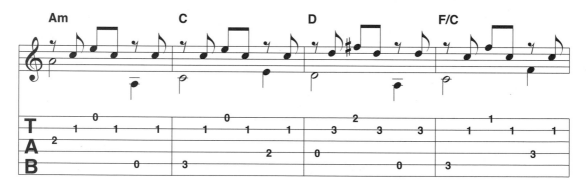

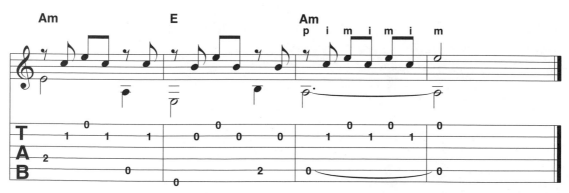

"Happy Birthday"

The previous arrangement of "House of the Rising Sun" had the melody at the bottom of the arrangement, played on strings 6, 5, 4, and 3. It is equally possible to play a melody at the top of an arrangement as the following version of "Happy Birthday" shows. First of all, here are the chords to "Happy Birthday."

$\frac{4}{4}$ A7///A7///A7///D//|D//|G//|D/A7|D//:‖

Next, here's the melody with corresponding words.

The sign over the B note in bar 6 is called a *fermata* and means pause on this note.

The next arrangement combines the chords and melody and is intended to be played with the pick. Make sure the melody—the highest note in each chord—is clearly audible.

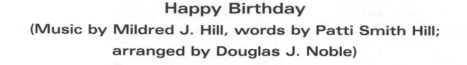

Happy Birthday
(Music by Mildred J. Hill, words by Patti Smith Hill; arranged by Douglas J. Noble)

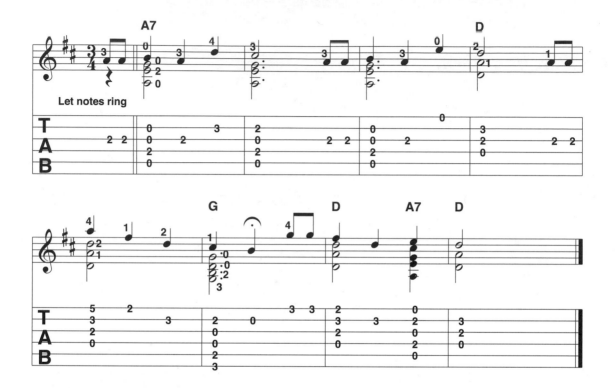

Résumé

You have now learned all fifteen of the basic open chord shapes— E, E7, Em, F, G, G7, A, A7, Am, B7, C, C7, D, D7, and Dm. If you cannot remember any of these chords, go back and memorize them!

You should know what is meant by *barré,* partial *barré,* triplet, and slash chord. You should be able to play arrangements of "House Of The Rising Sun" and "Happy Birthday" that combine the melody and chords.

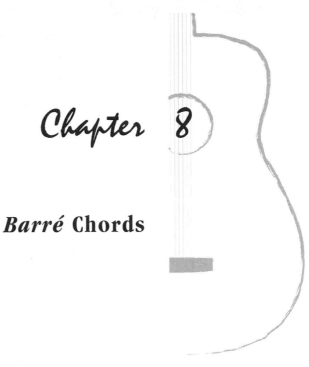

Chapter 8

Barré Chords

What are *Barré* Chords?

Now that we have learned the fifteen basic open chords, you may have noticed that some chords are missing. For example, we've learned the A and the C chords, but you may be wondering where's the B chord? We've learned Am and Dm, but why no Cm chord? The reason is that these chord shapes do not use any of the open strings, so they are not included in the open chord shapes. These chords consist entirely of fretted notes and the most efficient way to fret several notes at the same time is to use a *barré*. As we learned in the C, C7, and F Chords section of Chapter 7 (page 74), a **barré** is when a finger of the left hand—usually the 1st finger—is used to hold down two or more notes, usually on adjacent strings. *Barré* chords are often called *barre* chords or bar chords—we'll stick to *barré*.

Barré chords have the ability to strike fear into the heart of many a novice guitarist. Why? 'Cause they're very difficult, buddy... however, if you've conscientiously worked through this book and practiced regularly, you ought to be ready to tackle *barré* chords. Be forewarned though, they will take a lot of practice! Legend has it that American folk singer/songwriter Joni Mitchell found the F *barré* chord so difficult she resorted to tuning the guitar in a different way to avoid playing the F chord!

Barré chords are an essential part of the guitarist's musical vocabulary. The most common chord shapes in *barré* form are E,

E7, Em, A, A7, and Am. Playing *barré* chords is least difficult (notice I didn't say easiest, 'cause they're not easy!) on an electric guitar because the strings are easiest to hold down. *Barré* chords on an acoustic guitar are particularly difficult, simply because the strings are difficult to press down, and slightly less tough on a classical guitar—despite the wider neck, the strings are easier to press down.

The E Chord, *Barré*

In order to *barré* the E chord shape, E must be re-fingered with fingers 2, 3, and 4 instead of the usual 1, 2, and 3. This would make the E chord:

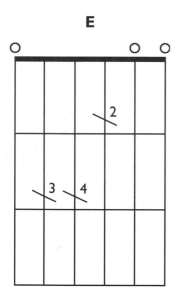

This fingering leaves the 1st finger free for the *barré*. Now, move this chord shape with fingers 2, 3, and 4 up a fret, which produces the F Spanish chord from Chapter 3's The E Chord section (page 36) then place the 1st finger across all six strings at the 1st fret, thus:

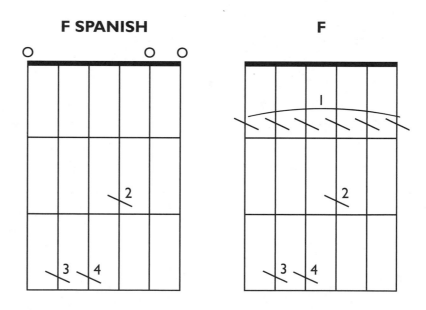

Remember to keep fingers 2, 3, and 4 smoothly curved, and instead of placing the thumb behind the 2nd finger move it slightly closer to the 1st finger, roughly halfway between the 1st and 2nd fingers—the 1st finger needs more support when playing *barré* chords. Play through the chord one note at a time and listen to each note—we want each note to sound clearly.

You should be able to work out from the Music Reading Fundamentals section in Chapter 2 (page 20) that the lowest note in the F chord—the bottom string 1st fret—is an F note. Just as with the open chords, the lowest note in a *barré* chord in its simplest form gives the chord its letter name. So, if, when fingering the F chord, you move the shape up one more fret (so the lowest note is the bottom string 2nd fret) the chord becomes F♯ or G♭—it's the same chord, just named differently. Similarly, move this shape up another fret so the lowest note is the bottom string 3rd fret and you have produced a G chord, thus:

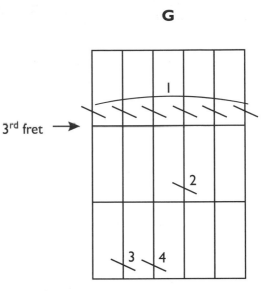

Compare the sounds of the open G chord and the *barré* G chord. Both chords consist entirely of G, B, and D notes (there will be more on chord theory in Chapter 9) and thus have a similar "overall" sound. However, there is a difference in "texture" and "tone."

You can continue moving this shape up the fretboard, producing a different major chord at each fret. Since there are twelve different letter names for notes, you can produce twelve different chords from the one chord shape. This is the beauty of *barré* chords—one chord shape can produce twelve different chords by playing it at different frets.

No doubt you found the F *barré* chord very tricky, but as you moved up the fretboard it should have become slightly easier as the frets become closer together. For practice we'll look at a chord progression using *barré* chords higher up the fretboard, namely the A and B chords.

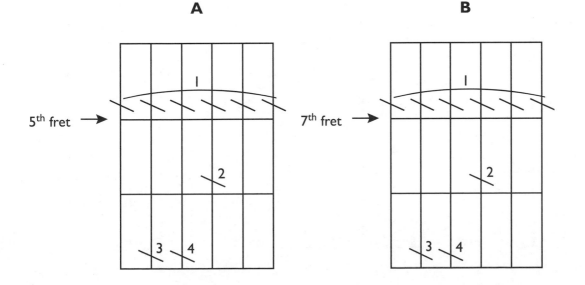

In the following chord progression, finger the E chord with fingers 2, 3, and 4 in preparation for the change to A—use fingers 2, 3, and 4 as guide fingers.

$\frac{4}{4}$ E///IA///IB///IA///:IIE

This is a very common chord progression and appears in various forms in The Troggs' "Wild Thing," Booker T. and The MG's "Soul Limbo," and The Kingsmen's "Louie, Louie."

E7 and Em *Barré* Shapes

The E7 shape is played with fingers 2 and 3 when playing *barré*. As we did with the E chord shape, start with E7 at the bottom of the fretboard then move fingers 2 and 3 up by one fret, to frets 3 and 2, respectively, on strings 5 and 3. When playing the 1st fret *barré,* this produces an F7 chord. Move the chord up the fretboard one fret at a time, naming each chord as you play it—remember, this chord takes its letter name from the lowest note in the chord, that is, the note on the bottom string. As with the E chord *barré* shape, this chord gets slightly easier as it is moved up the fretboard and the frets get closer together. Opposite you can see the F7, A7, and B7 *barré* chords.

The trickiest note to get clearly is the note on the 4th string—the *barré* must be held down firmly in order to get a clear note. Try not to position the 1st finger so that the natural "folds" in the

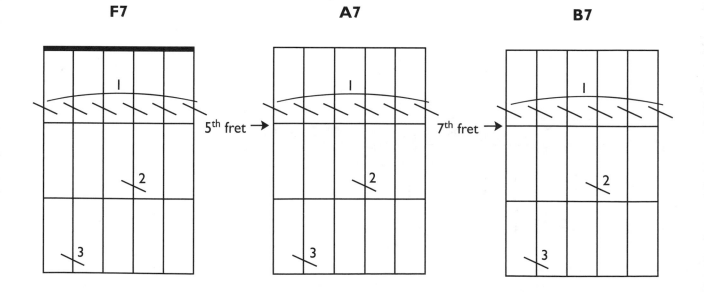

finger are pressing the strings down—it's difficult to get a clear note that way. A slight adjustment of the finger, either upwards or downwards, will prevent this. Everyone's fingers are different, so some experimentation is necessary. Here's a progression similar to the previous one for practicing these *barré* 7 shapes (finger E7 with fingers 2 and 3):

$\frac{4}{4}$ E7///|A7///|B7///|A7///:||E7

For further practice, go back to Chapter 5 and play the two chord progressions in The Twelve-Bar Blues Progression section (page 45) using these *barré* shapes.

In order to prepare the Em chord to barré, it has to be re-fingered with fingers 3 and 4 instead of 2 and 3. Below are the chord diagrams for Fm, Am, and Bm using the Em shape.

Fm   Am   Bm

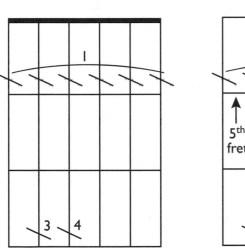
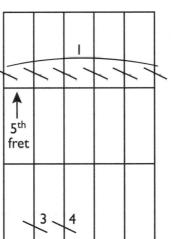
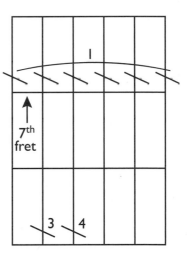

Here's a chord progression using these chords.

$\frac{4}{4}$ Em///|Am///|Bm///|Am///:||Em

A, A7, and Am *Barré* Shapes

In Chapter 7 we played two versions of the A chord, both containing the same notes but using different left-hand fingers (see page 73). In order to prepare the A chord for *barré,* it is necessary to finger it with fingers 2, 3, and 4, leaving the 1st finger free for the *barré.* The A chord is a five-string chord, the lowest note being the open 5th string which gives the A chord its letter name. Moving the whole shape up by one fret and playing *barré* at the 1st fret means it takes its letter name from the 5th string 1st fret, which is a B♭ note. Here are these A and B♭ chord shapes:

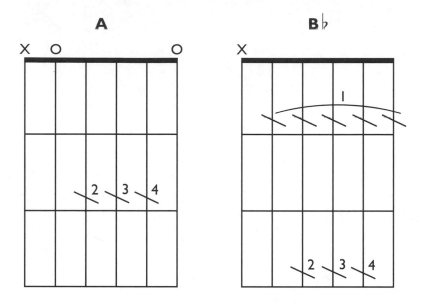

You'll probably notice that it's quite a squeeze to get fingers 2, 3, and 4 all behind the 3rd fret for B♭. Many players alter this fingering, replacing fingers 2, 3, and 4 with a *barré* with the 3rd finger, thus:

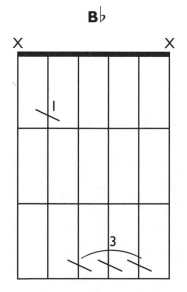

Notice the top string is now missed out from the chord shape. Since it is tricky to avoid sounding this string when strumming this chord, the 3rd finger is used to touch the top string lightly to deaden it so that when this string is hit it doesn't produce a note. If your 3rd finger is double-jointed you can place it in such a way as to rise above the top string then do a *barré* with the 1st finger producing a five-note chord, thus:

DOUBLE JOINTED B♭

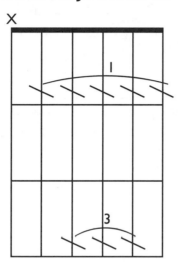

However, few people can manage such finger contortions and most stick to the four-string version. Here are D and E *barré* chords using the A chord shape:

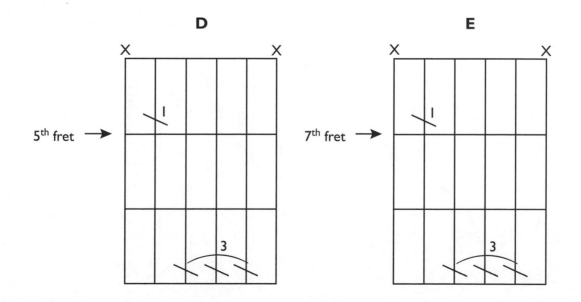

Use these D and E shapes in the following progression, and start with an A *barré* chord using the E chord shape.

$\frac{4}{4}$ A///|D///|E///|D///:||A

By now, the principle behind *barré* chords should be clear. The two remaining shapes to *barré* are A7 and Am. Open A7 has to be re-fingered with fingers 3 and 4 instead of 2 and 4 in preparation for playing *barré*. Here's the chord re-fingered in preparation for this technique, followed by B♭7 and E7 *barré* chords using the A7 shape.

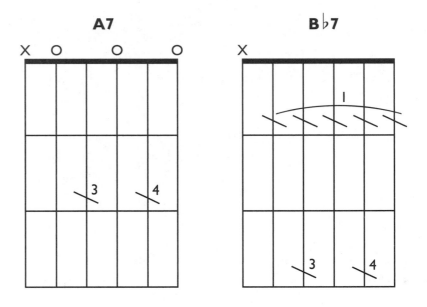

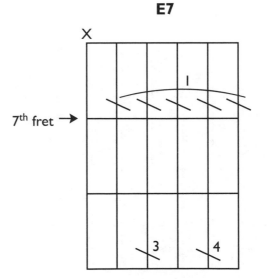

Similarly, here's the re-fingered Am chord, followed by B♭m and Dm *barré* chords using the Am shape.

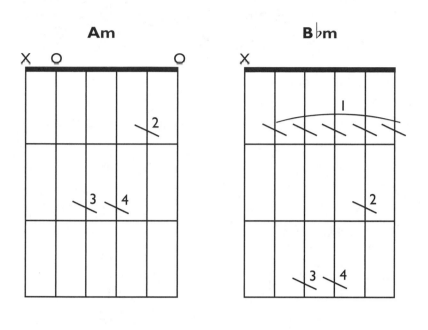

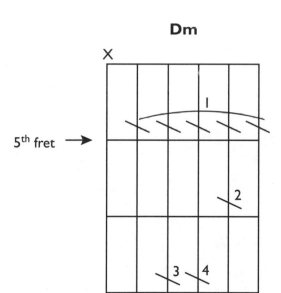

Finally, a chord progression bringing together these E7 and Dm shapes. Start with the Am *barré* chord based on the Em shape.

$\frac{4}{4}$ Am///|Dm///|E7///|Dm///:||Am

The Five-Chord Voicing Method

Although the E, E7, Em, A, A7, and Am chords are the most commonly major chord shapes in *barré*, it is also possible to *barré* the open G, C, and D chords. Using all five basic open major chord shapes it is possible to play any major chord in five different positions. Working up the fretboard, the shapes used would be E, G, A, C, and D; play these in turn and notice how the lowest notes of these chords ascend. As with when we *barré* the E chord, *barrés* with the G, A, C, and D chord shapes require re-fingering the basic shape without finger 1 in order to leave it free for the *barré*.

Below is the F chord played in five different positions using these five chord shapes.

'F' (E shape)

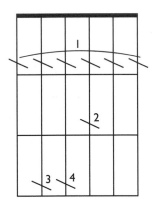

'F' (D shape)

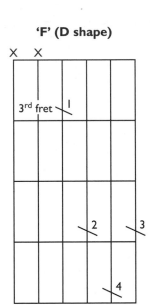

'F' (C shape)

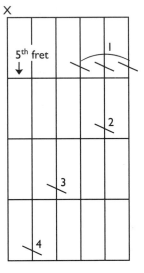

'F' (A shape)

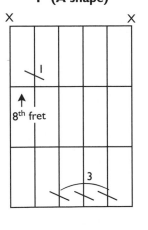

'F' (G shape)

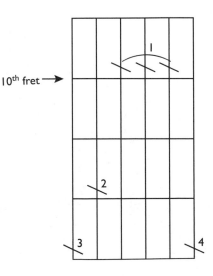

It should now be apparent why the E and A chords are the shapes most commonly used for *barré*—the other *barré* shapes are awkward for the fingers! Notice how the second of these shapes, based on the D chord, is not actually a *barré* chord—the 1st finger only has to hold down one note, so there is no need for a *barré*.

This is a useful exercise for understanding the principle behind *barré* chords and for improving one's technique for playing *barré* chords—in practice, the *barré* chords based on the G, C, and D chords are rarely used.

There are only three open minor chords—Em, Am, and Dm—so the equivalent exercise for minor chords has only three different positions. Here are three different versions of Fm using the Em, Am, and Dm chord shapes:

'Fm' in 3 Different Positions

'Fm' (Em shape)

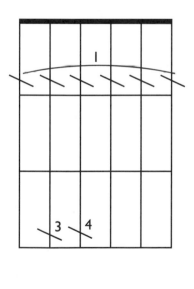

'Fm' (Dm shape)

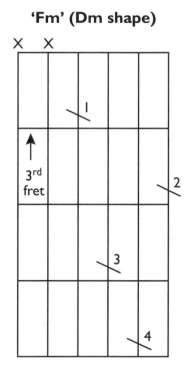

'Fm' (Am shape)

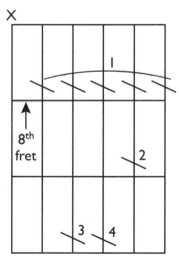

Notice, once again, that the second version of Fm, which uses the Dm chord shape, does not require a *barré* since the 1st finger only has to hold down one string.

Progression Using *Barré* Chords

There follows a progression using *barré* chord shapes. For this first progression, the '50s pop progression from Chapter 7's Three

Standard Chord Progressions (page 75), use the A chord shape for
E, the Am chord shape for C#m, the E chord shape for A, and the
E7 chord shape for B7.

$$\frac{4}{4} \text{E}///\text{IC}\sharp\text{m}///\text{IA}///\text{IB7}///:\text{IIE}$$

Here's a more interesting way to play this progression involving *arpeggio* chords and a bass run in the 4th bar.

Arpeggio Progression Using *Barré* Chords

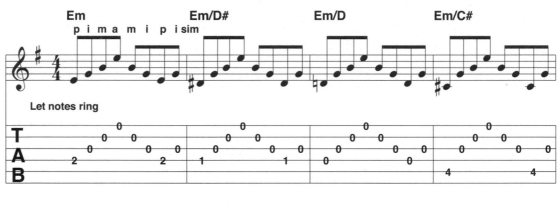

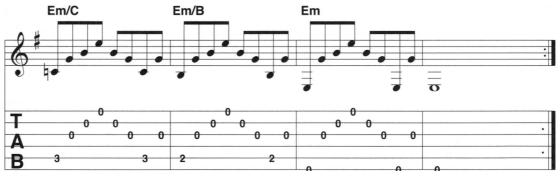

Résumé

You should now understand the principle behind *barré* chords.
You should practice the *barré* chord shapes based on the open
shapes of E, E7, Em, A, A7, and Am, starting at the bottom of the
fretboard and moving up one fret at a time, naming each chord as
you play it. Since *barré* chords are easier to play when the frets
are closer together, practice the chord progressions covered in this
chapter that deliberately avoid the *barré* shapes at the bottom of
the fretboard.

Chapter 9

Music Theory

Why Learn Music Theory?

Strictly speaking, there is no need to learn music theory in order to play the guitar, just as there is no need to learn how to read music. However, many beginners will have questions about many of the topics covered so far in this book, particularly about chords. What's the difference between a major and a minor chord? Why are there different versions of the same chord? (We have encountered four different versions of the G chord so far.) Such questions can only be answered after covering some basic music theory. Learning music theory will not necessarily make you a better player, but many guitarists find that it increases their confidence if they understand what they are playing. The theory in this chapter is all practically-based, that is, it is all about something guitarists play every day: chords.

The C Major Scale

In order to understand chords, we have to learn a scale, since the notes in scales are the building blocks for chords. Most of the theory in this chapter will be based on the C major scale. Here's a one-octave fingering for the C major scale—"octave" means it starts on C and proceeds up to the next C note. Since C is the starting note, we call C the "root" note of the scale. Notice that the notes of the scale have been numbered—this is important for the following section.

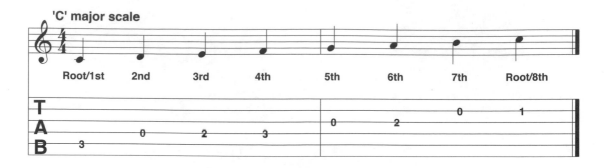

Triads—Three-Note Chords

In the beginning, there was the major scale. From this scale we can form chords. To form a chord from the C major scale we take the root note (or 1st note), the 3rd note, and the 5th note—so the basic formula is root/1st, 3rd, and 5th. These three notes are called a "triad"—"tri" meaning "three." You can see from the scale in the previous section that these notes are C, E, and G. If you play these notes individually, you have a C major triad *arpeggio;* play them simultaneously and you have a C major triad chord.

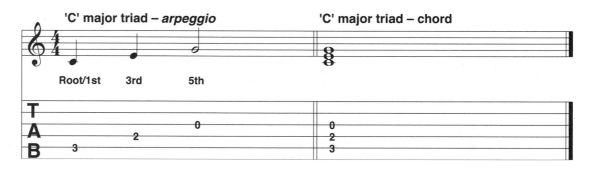

There are three other types of triad. The formula for a minor triad is root, flattened 3rd (also known as the minor 3rd), and 5th. To "flatten" a note you move it down (that is, lower in pitch) by one fret. Flatten the 3rd from the C major scale, and E becomes E♭. Here are the C minor triad *arpeggio* and chord:

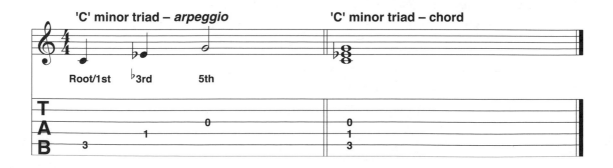

So, whether a chord—and for that matter, a scale—is major or minor is determined by what type of "3rd" it contains. If it contains a major 3rd (that is, the 3rd as it occurs in the major scale) it is a major chord or scale; if it contains a minor, or flattened, 3rd it is a minor chord or scale. Here's an exercise consisting of the first three notes of the C major scale followed by a C major triad chord, then the first three notes of the C minor scale followed by a C minor triad chord. Play slowly, listen closely, and hear the difference between major and minor.

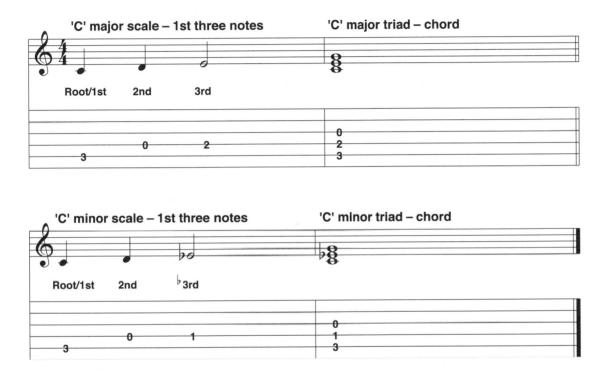

The other two types of triad are augmented and diminished, but in general, these types of chords are rarely encountered. The formula for the augmented triad is root/1st, 3rd, and sharpened 5th. To sharpen a note you move it up (that is, higher in pitch) by one fret. Here's the C augmented triad *arpeggio* and chord:

Finally, the C diminished triad. The formula for this is root/1st, flattened 3rd, and flattened 5th. The flattened 3rd is E♭. The 5th in the C major scale is the open G note; to flatten this would make G♭. Since it is impossible to play this note on the 3rd string from our current position, the chord requires some note juggling, resulting in the following C diminished triad chord:

Notice that the diminished triad contains a flattened 3rd, which would make it a minor triad, but because it also contains a flattened 5th, the diminished triad can be thought of as a special kind of minor triad. The diminished triad can also be called a min♭5 chord.

Forming Chords from Triads

As already explained, a triad consists of three notes. On the guitar we obviously have more than three strings, so how do we make a triad into a chord shape that suits the guitar? The answer is simple, we just double the notes in other octaves. So, since the C major triad consists of C, E, and G, we just add other C, E, and G notes. There's no theoretical reason for which of these notes to choose—we simply add whichever notes fall conveniently under the fingers. Strings 5, 4, and 3 are already occupied with C, E, and G notes, respectively, so we can add another C note on the 2nd string 1st fret and another E as the open top string. And what do you know, this gives us the conventional C chord:

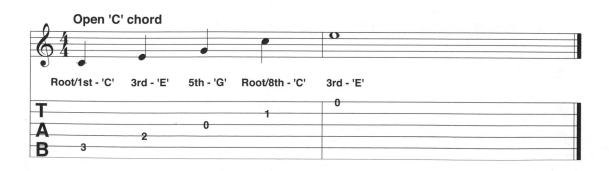

You might realize that there is a G note on the top string at the 3rd fret that could be used. This would also make the C chord:

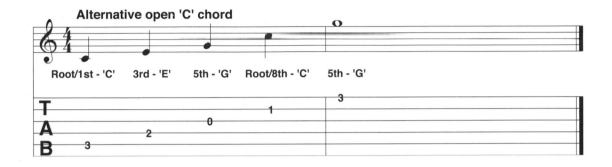

Both are equally correct and valid C chords, but the first version is slightly easier since it uses three fingers instead of four, which is partly why it has been adopted as the standard open C chord. Because they contain the same notes but in a slightly different arrangement, these chords are called different "voicings." Since all that a C major chord consists of is a collection of C, E, and G notes, you should be able to see that it is possible to play many different voicings of the C chord. That's why there is no naming system to distinguish between them—there are simply too many possibilities.

We'll demonstrate transforming a triad into a chord in another key—the key of G. Here's a one-octave G major scale with degrees of the scale indicated:

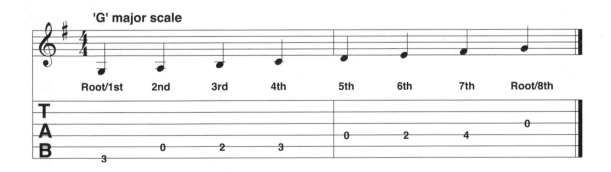

Using the formula root/1st, 3rd, and 5th, gives us the following notes:

You can work out that the G triad consists of the notes G, B, and D. In order to make the triad into a six-note guitar chord we just double these notes in other octaves. Conveniently we have an open G note on the 3rd string. We can add a D on the 2nd string 3rd fret. On the top string, the only one of these three notes that is playable is the G—top string 3rd fret. This gives the guitar chord as:

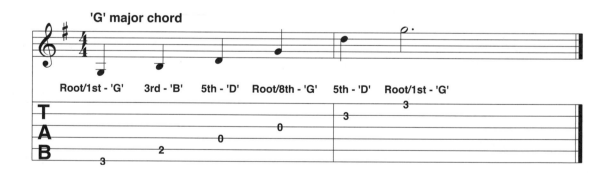

Remember: the G chord can also be fingered by playing the open 2nd string instead of playing the 2nd string at the 3rd fret—this gives a B note.

E5 and E6 Chords

In Chapter 5 (page 47) you were told that the E5 chord consists of an E note plus the fifth note of the E major scale and the E6 chord consists of an E note plus the sixth note of the E major scale. Now let's prove it! Here's a one-octave E major scale.

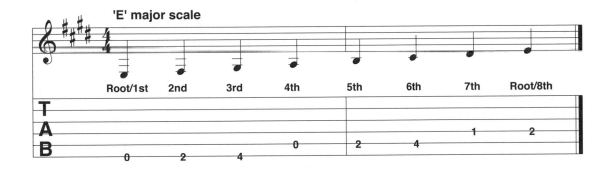

Below are the 1st and 5th notes played separately from the scale, followed by them played simultaneously which produces the E5 chord you learned in Chapter 5, then the 1st and 6th notes played separately from the scale followed by the E6 chord, also learned in Chapter 5.

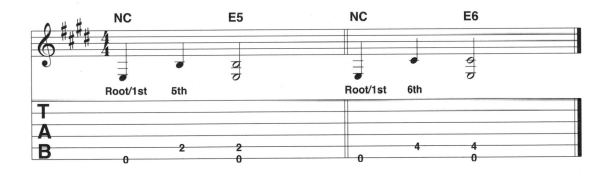

Notice that these 5 and 6 chords do not contain the 3rd degree of the scale. We have already learned that it is this 3rd note of the scale that makes the chord major or minor. Hence, these 5 and 6 chords are neither major nor minor. The 5 chord is particularly interesting—listen closely to E5 and hear how it has a very "bare" and "open" sound. The 5 chord is particularly versatile and is used a lot by rock guitarists. Here are two progressions, the first played in open chords, the second being basically the same as the first but played in power chords.

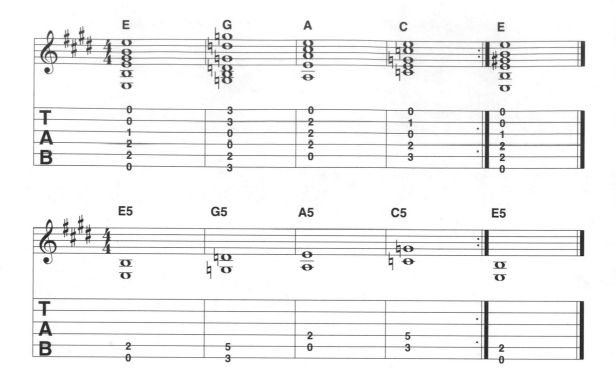

Dominant 7th Chord

We have already seen how major and minor chords are formed, but what about 7th chords, or dominant 7th chords, to give them their full name? The formula for a dominant 7th chord is root/1st, 3rd, 5th, and flattened 7th. If you look back to the C major scale at the beginning of this chapter (page 96) you'll see that the 7th note of the C major scale is B. If we flatten this note (that is, make it lower by one fret) we get B♭. So, a C7 chord consists of the notes C, E, G, and B♭. Here's the C7 shape we've already learned showing this:

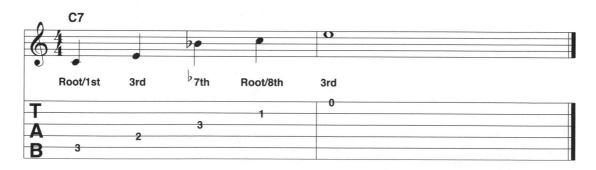

Note that this chord has no 5th—no G note. It is permitted to omit the 5th of a chord and the chord remains unaltered; omitting the 3rd or root/1st would change the chord.

Now we have looked at how the three main types of chords are formed—major, minor, and 7th.

Chord Families and Roman Numeral Chord Notation

We have already discussed that in music there are keys that consist of families of chords that work together. Now we will look at how these "chord families" are formed.

First, we need to extend the C major scale to include the next five notes in the second octave, as shown below.

We have already seen in the earlier Triads—Three Note Chords section (page 96) that by taking the root/1st, 3rd, and 5th we form a C major triad. Then, in the Forming Chords from Triads section (page 98) we saw that by doubling the same notes in other octaves we arrived at the basic open C chord. Here are the 1st, 3rd, and 5th, followed by the triad, followed by the basic open C chord:

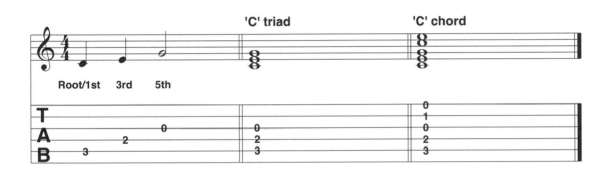

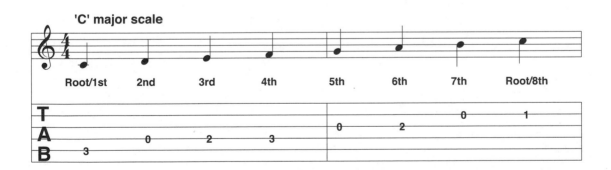

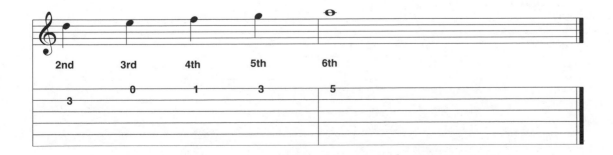

Since this chord is formed from the first note of the major scale, it is represented by the Roman numeral I. So, chord I refers to the chord built on the 1st note of any major scale, which is always a major chord.

To work out which chords work alongside this C chord we take the 2nd note in the C major scale, D. We now think of this note as being the root/1st note of a triad and pick out the 3rd and 5th notes above it—the 3rd note is F and the 5th note is A. Relative to the D note, the formula of this is root/1st, ♭3rd, and 5th—this forms a minor triad. Rearranging the notes into a more "guitar-friendly" chord and doubling the D note to make use of the top four strings, we end up with the basic open Dm chord thus:

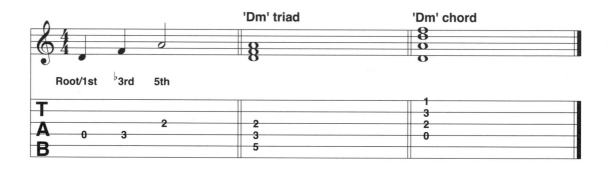

Since this chord was built on the 2nd note of the major scale it is represented by the Roman numeral II. Chord II is always minor.

Next, we take the 3rd note of the C major scale and treat this as the root/1st—this is an E note. The 3rd note up from that is G and the 5th is B. These notes form an Em triad. Rearranging the notes we get the basic open Em chord:

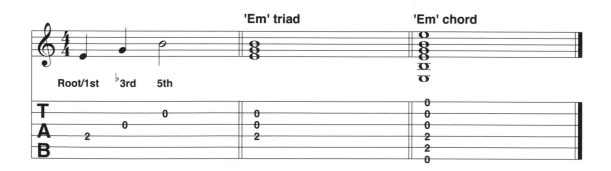

Since this chord was built on the 3rd note of the major scale it is represented by the Roman numeral III. Chord III is always minor.

We now move on to the 4th note in the C major scale, F. Treating F as the root/1st note of a triad, the 3rd is A and the 5th is C. These notes form a major triad, chord IV, which is always major. Rearranging them, we get the F *barré* chord:

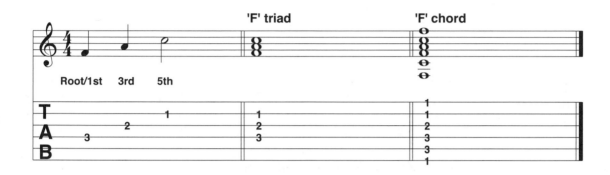

You are hopefully getting the idea by now! Next, we take the 5th note in the C major scale, G. Treating G as the root/1st note of a triad, the 3rd is B, and the fifth is D. This chord built on the 5th degree of the scale, chord V, is often extended to include the 7th, which in this case would be F. This produces a four-note chord—with a big stretch!—that is rearranged to form the basic open G7 chord shown below.

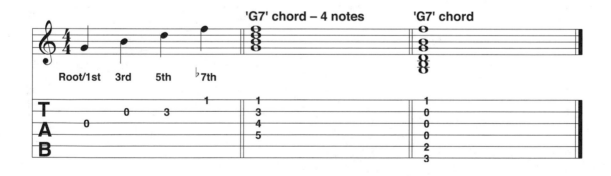

If the chord built on the 5th degree of the major scale is restricted to three notes it is a major chord and known as chord V; if it includes the 7th it is known as chord V7.

We now take the 6th degree of the major scale, A. Treating this as the root, the 3rd is C and the 5th is E. This gives us a minor triad, and the notes can be rearranged to form the basic open Am chord thus:

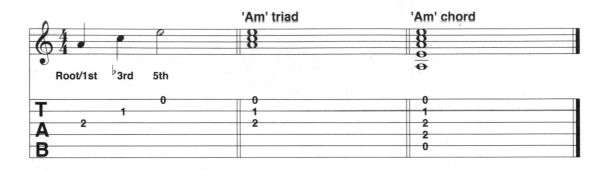

Chord VII Is Always Minor

Next, we take the 7th note of the major scale, B. Treating this as the root note, the 3rd is D and the 5th is F. This forms a diminished triad. However, chord VII is often extended to include the 7th, which in this case would be an A note. This forms a minor 7♭5 chord. Here's how we arrive at the four-note version of the chord:

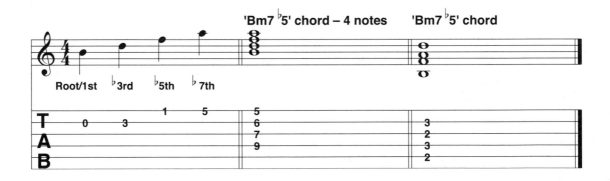

If this chord contains three notes it is referred to as chord VII and is a diminished chord; if it contains four notes it is referred to as chord VII7 and is a min7♭5 chord. This chord built on the 7th degree of the scale occurs only infrequently, and is perhaps more used in its four-note form than its three-note form. On the following page are three movable fingerings for the min7♭5 chord with root notes on strings 6, 5, and 4:

m7♭5 – ROOT ON ⑥

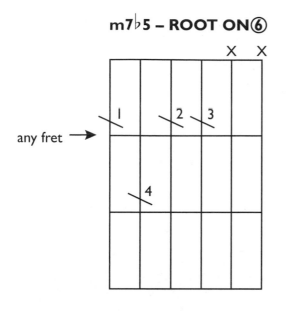

any fret →

m7♭5 – ROOT ON ⑤

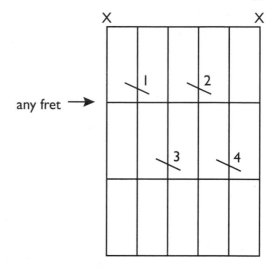

any fret →

The next note in the C major scale is a C note, so we're back to where we started. To summarize, whatever major key you are in, chord I is major, chord II is minor, chord III is minor, chord IV is major, chord V(7) is major or a dominant 7th if the 7th is included, chord VI is minor, chord VII(7) is a minor7♭5 in its four-note version. The purpose of Roman numeral chord notation is that chord progressions can be referred to in general terms without reference to a specific key. For example, the '50s pop progression from Chapter 7's Three Standard Chord Progressions section (page 75) can be referred to as a I/VI/IV/V. We will use this Roman numeral chord notation in Chapter 12, Jazz.

m7♭5 – ROOT ON ④

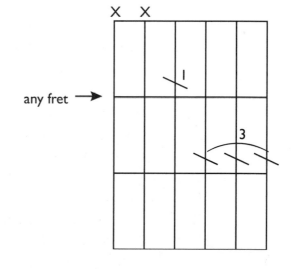

any fret →

Here are the "chord scales" in the five most common major keys on the guitar. Using your knowledge of the fifteen basic open chords, *barré* chord shapes from Chapter 8 and the three min7♭5 chords you have just learned, you should be able to play through all of these progressions.

In the key of C:

$\frac{4}{4}$ *C/// | Dm/// | Em/// | F/// | G(7)/// | Am/// | Bm7♭5/// | C///: | |*

In the key of D:

$\frac{4}{4}$ *D/// | Em/// | F♯m/// | G/// | A(7)/// | Bm/// | C♯m7♭5/// | D///: | |*

In the key of E:

$\frac{4}{4}$ *E/// | F♯m/// | G♯m/// | A/// | B(7)/// | C♯m/// | D♯m7♭5/// | E///: | |*

In the key of G:

$\frac{4}{4}$ *G/// | Am/// | Bm/// | C/// | D(7)/// | Em/// | F♯m7♭5/// | G///: | |*

In the key of A:

$\frac{4}{4}$ *A/// | Bm/// | C♯m/// | D/// | E(7)/// | F♯m/// | G♯m7♭5/// | A///: | |*

In practice, if a song sticks to these chords in a particular key, the overall effect will be rather bland and uninteresting, so most venture into other keys at some point to add tension and spice.

Résumé

You should understand the terms "triad" and "voicing." You should know what a triad is, how it is formed, what the four different kinds of triads are, and how they are converted to chords for the guitar. You should be able to play the "chord scales" in the most common guitar keys of C, D, E, G, and A, and understand how they are formed.

Chapter 10

The Blues Scale

The E Blues Scale

The blues scale is the most commonly used scale in blues and also rock music, and it is even occasionally used in jazz. The particular pattern of the E blues scale we are going to look at is often known as the 1st position blues scale. The use of the word "position" in guitar playing can be confusing since it can have two meanings. In classical guitar usage, position refers to which fret the 1st finger is at. Since the fingers are kept one-finger-per-fret, this automatically determines which frets the other fingers are at. For example, playing in the 3rd position means the 1st finger is at the 3rd fret, therefore the 2nd finger is at the 4th fret, the 3rd finger at the 5th fret, and the 4th finger at the 6th fret. When talking about the blues scales, position usually refers to a specific pattern of the scale, although this naming is not standardized or universal. It just so happens that with this 1st position E blues scale the 1st finger is actually used at the 1st fret, but this is coincidence. If the notes in this 1st position E blues

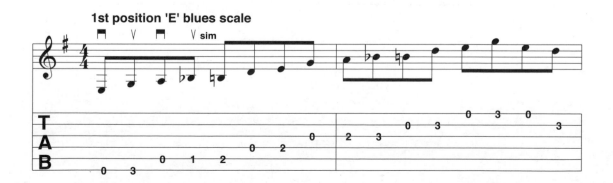

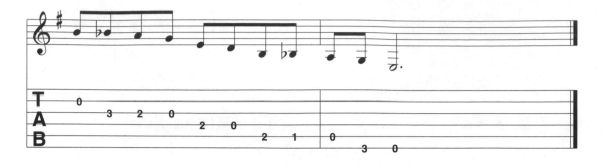

scale were all moved up an octave—that is, twelve frets higher—it would still be known as the 1st position E blues scale.

This is how this scale would be written in a fretboard diagram, first at the bottom of the fretboard and then twelve frets higher. Remember, both scales are called the 1st position E blues scale. The blues scale is sometimes referred to as a "box position" scale because all the notes are contained within a one-finger-per-fret area of the fretboard.

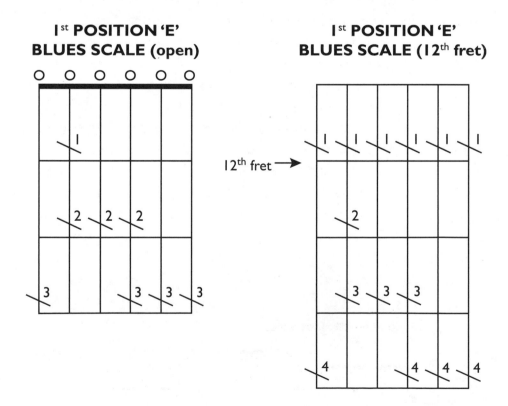

To derive the formula for a scale we compare each of the notes with the equivalent note in the major scale, which, as we have already seen in Chapter 9 (page 96), has the formula "root/1st, 2nd, 3rd, 4th, 5th, 6th, 7th, root/8th."

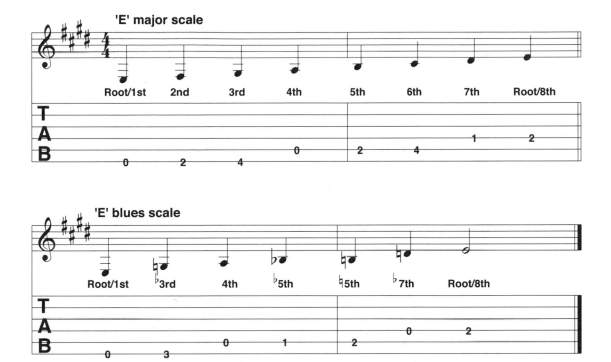

Both scales start with the root note, or 1st note, of E. Looking at the music, notice there is no F♯ or F-natural, signified by the ♮ sign, in the E blues scale, so there is no "2nd" in the blues scale. The blues scale contains a G♮ compared with a G♯ or "3rd" in the major scale; to denote this fact the G♮ is denoted as ♭3rd. Comparing note with note, the formula for the E blues scale is therefore "root/1st, ♭3rd, 4th, ♭5th, 5th, ♭7th, root/8th." Notice that, just as there is no 2nd degree of the scale, neither is there a 6th degree—there's no C♯ or C in the blues scale.

The term "blues notes" is generally used to refer to the notes that give the blues scale its characteristic sound or "mood." While the ♭3rd and ♭7th both shape the scale's flavor, it's the ♭5th degree of the scale that sounds the most striking note in the scale.

The blues scale is closely related to the pentatonic minor scale, which, as the name suggests, is a five-note scale ("pent" means five) with a minor third. To convert the blues scale into the pentatonic minor, simply omit the ♭5th—B♭ in the E blues scale. Hence, the E pentatonic minor scale is:

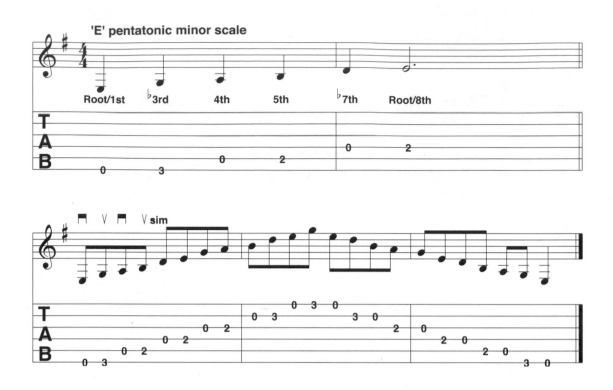

Some 1st Position E Blues Scale Licks

A "lick" is a general name for a short, melodic phrase found in blues, jazz, and country music. We will work on four licks then join them together in a twelve-bar blues progression. Practice these licks by playing each one over and over again, back to back. Blues lead playing often uses "bends," "slides," "hammer-ons," and "pull-offs" to make the music more articulate and expressive (keep reading, all will be explained!). These licks deliberately avoid using bends so they can be played on classical, acoustic, and electric guitars—bends are very difficult (almost impossible, in fact) on classical and acoustic guitars.

The first lick begins with a slide on the 3rd string from the 2nd fret to the 4th fret. A slide is indicated in music notation and tablature by the letter "S" and a diagonal line showing the direction of the slide—that is, if the line slopes upwards from left to right then the slide moves from a lower note to a higher note, as in this case; if the line slopes downwards from left to right then the slide is from a higher note to a lower note. The small note at the beginning is called an *acciaccatura*—this is a grace note played as quickly as possible. So, as soon as you have sounded this note on the 3rd string 2nd fret, slide up two frets to the 4th fret. In order to get a clear slide, the 2nd finger must be kept firmly on the string.

Notice that the *acciaccatura* grace note is connected to the second note by a curved line—this is called a "slur." A slur joins together two notes of different pitches and means the second of the two notes is not plucked. The second note can either be slid into (either up or down) or sounded with a hammer-on or pull-off (more on these shortly).

Notice the pick directions: down-down-down, up-down-up, then downstrokes for the E5 chord. The timing is two triplets of single notes followed by four strikes of the E5 chord in the shuffle rhythm. Phonetically this would sound like: "di-di-di, di-di-di, duuh du, duuh du." Which left-hand fingers to use are indicated beside the notes in the music.

Lick I

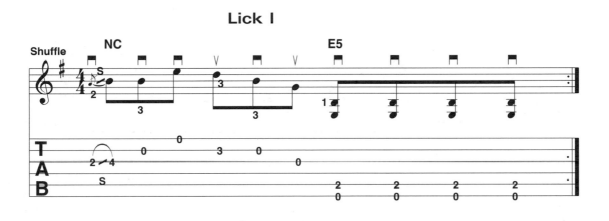

This next lick begins with a run up the first five notes of the E blues scale. Strict alternate picking is used for the single notes, and the timing is the same as the previous lick—"di-di-di, di-di-di, duuh du, duuh du."

Lick II

The third lick begins with a hammer-on. This is indicated by the slur joining the *acciaccatura* grace note and the first main note. To execute the slur, first pluck the open D string then bring the 2nd finger of the left hand firmly down on the 4th string at the 2nd fret. The note produced by a slur has a softer attack than when plucking the note with a pick or a finger. The opposite of a hammer-on is a pull-off. To pull-off to the open 4th string from the 2nd fret, place the 2nd finger on the 4th string 2nd fret, pluck the note, then pull the finger downwards towards the 3rd string—this will sound the open 4th string, and can be thought of as plucking the string with the left-hand 2nd finger.

Since the hammer-on is executed as quickly as possible, the timing of this lick is essentially the same as the previous lick—"di-di-di, di-di-di, duuh du, duuh du."

Lick III

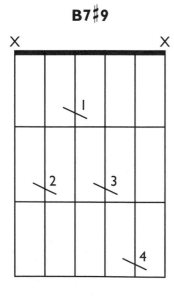

B7♯9

The final lick is a turnaround (we previously encountered a turnaround in the Shuffle Variations section on page 52 of Chapter 5) and uses B7♯9:

This chord sounds very striking and rather "dissonant"—which means there's a clash between notes in the chord, in this case between the D♯ on the 4th string and the C✗ (C double sharp) on the 2nd string.

Notice the dot below the E5 chord at the beginning of this lick. This is a *staccato* dot—*staccato* means stop the chord as soon as you have played it. In this case this can be done by lifting the 1st finger from the 5th string then quickly stopping the bottom string by touching it with the fingers of the right hand; alternatively it is perhaps easier to bring the palm of the right hand firmly down onto the strings, stopping them dead.

After the *staccato* E5 chord, there's a series of triplets played with down-up-down pick directions. These are indicated to be played by leaving the 4th finger on the 5th string 7th fret and moving the 1st finger up the bottom string one fret at a time.

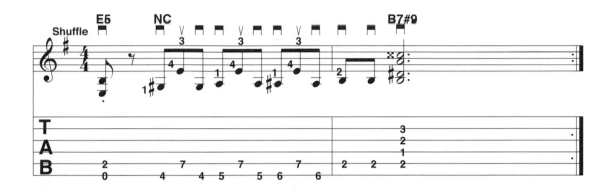

Two-Part Blues

The music on page 116 is called Two-Part Blues because it jumps from a "lead" lick to a chord on the bass strings. In rock and blues there is sometimes a distinction made between "lead" and "rhythm" guitarists in a band. The lead guitarist will play the single-note solos and any single-note fills between the vocalist's phrases, whereas the rhythm guitarist will provide the chords and riffs. (Unless they are particularly self-indulgent, lead guitarists will often spend more time playing rhythm than lead anyway, so lead guitarists ought to be good rhythm guitarists as well.) For example, the Rolling Stones' Keith Richards is a rhythm guitarist who rarely plays solos. As the lead guitarist in his own band, Carlos Santana has rhythm guitarists to play behind him when he solos; similarly blues guitarist and singer B.B. King is a lead guitarist who rarely plays chords at all.

Two-Part Blues uses the previous four 1st position E blues licks in a twelve-bar blues, the overall progression being the same as Shuffle Blues in E from Chapter 5 (page 46), although to keep the rhythm part straightforward (there's enough to think about!) the rhythm part sticks to 5 chords instead of 5 and 6 chords. To make the piece more interesting there are some variations on these licks. For example, in the second half of bar 3 and the first half of bar 4, the second lick is played verbatim, whereas in the second half of bar 4 the last note of this second lick is changed. Watch out for other variations.

Two-Part Blues

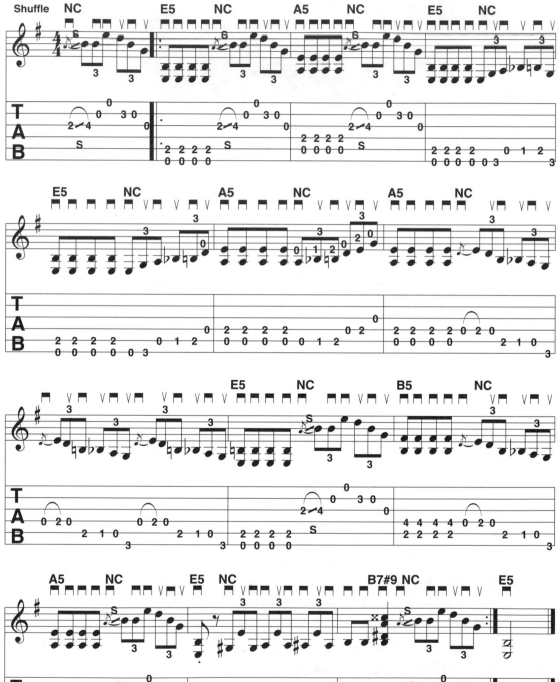

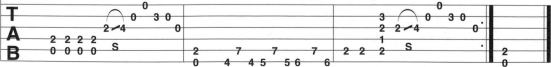

Résumé

You should know what is meant by *acciaccatura,* lick, slur, hammer-on and dissonant. Although the harmonic language of blues is very simple—put very simply, there's only one chord progression and only one scale—to play blues convincingly requires immersing yourself in the style by listening to as much as possible and by constantly refining your playing. There's some recommended listening in Discography (Chapter 13, page 143).

Chapter 11

Interesting-Sounding Chords and Progressions

At this point we have learned all the basic open chords and the most commonly used *barré* chords. Now we will look at some interesting-sounding and more harmonically-advanced chords which are not much more difficult to play than the basic open chords: the guitar lends itself to some very nice sounding chords.

The Movable Open E Chord

We have already seen in Chapter 3's E Chord section (page 36) how the open E chord shape can be moved up the fretboard to

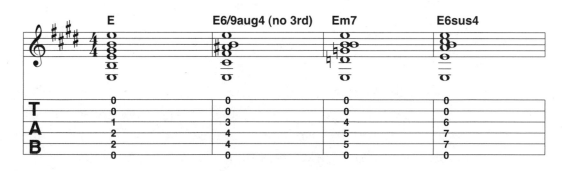

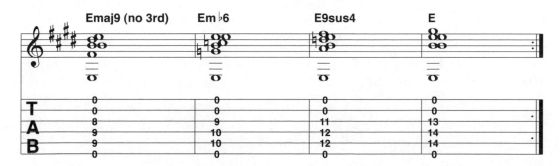

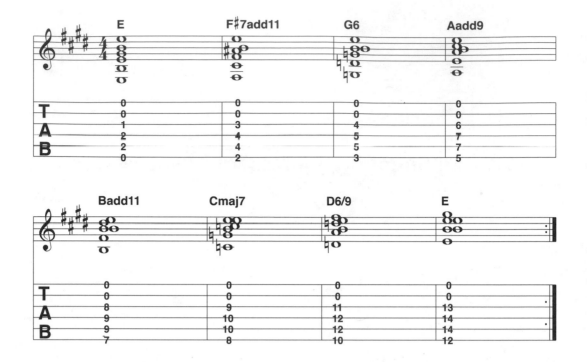

create what we call F Spanish and G Spanish chords. This idea is used in the previous chord progression to create some interesting and rich-sounding chords. No chord diagrams are needed because we are simply moving the basic open E chord up the fretboard.

Notice how the fretted notes in the last chord in the example above are an octave (eight scale notes, or twelve frets) higher than the first chord shape; both these chords are called E. A variation on this progression is to move the bass note on the bottom string with the chord shape. Listen to how this adds depth at the bottom of the chord, and notice how it also changes the chord names.

The sus4 and sus2 Chords

"Sus" is short for "suspended" and these two chords are so called because they sound "suspended," "unresolved," or "restless"—similar, in a sense, to a 7th chord. The D chord is often used in conjunction with sus4 and sus2 chords.

Try to hear how these chords sound different from a 7th chord. For example, you could hear a 7th chord as having a bluesy tinge to it, whereas the sus4 chord has a sweeter sound to it. The sus2 chord contains a mild dissonance, or clash, because the sus2 note is close to the root. Both Dsus4 and Dsus2 are resolved by following them with the D chord. Here is an exercise using these three chords (see the chords on the next page).

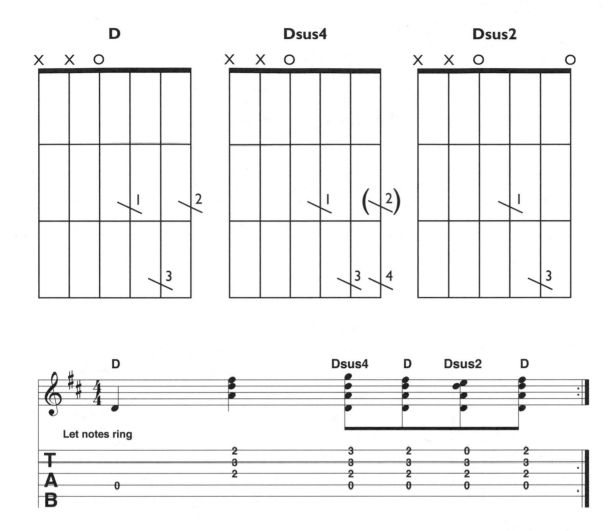

Similar progressions are occasionally encountered in the key of A, using A, Asus4, and Asus2 chords.

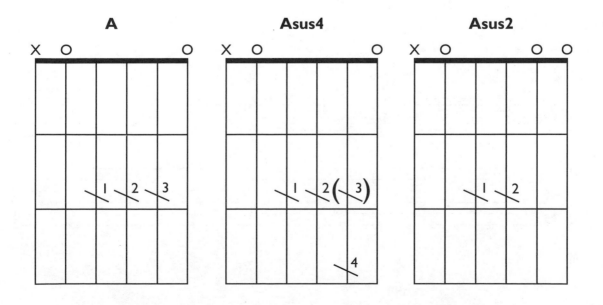

Here is the equivalent exercise using these three chords:

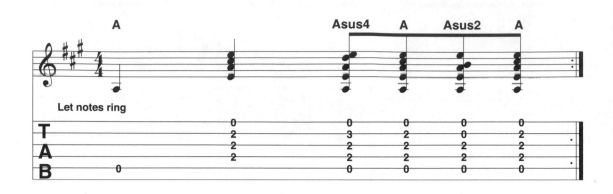

The "Hendrix Chord"

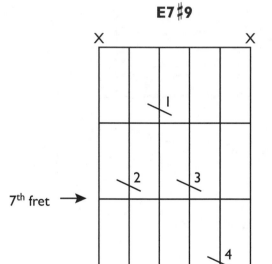

E7♯9

7th fret →

The 7♯9 chord is known by guitarists as the "Hendrix chord" since Jimi Hendrix popularized it in "Purple Haze." Hendrix made this chord part of the rock guitarist's chord vocabulary, although funk and jazz guitarists use it as well. We previously encountered this 7♯9 chord in Some 1st Position E Blues Scale Licks in Chapter 10 as B7♯9 (see page 114). Moving this shape up so the 2nd finger is at the 7th fret produces E7♯9:

Here's an exercise using the E7♯9 chord.

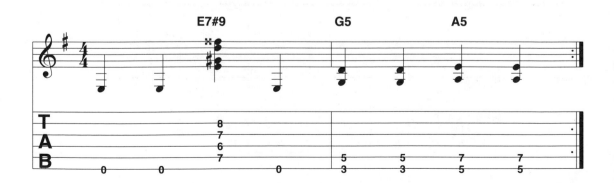

The 9th Chord

The 9th chord is used in funk music. Below is the most common voicing for the 9th chord, first as E9, then moving the shape up by one fret to produce an F9 chord. The tricky part in this chord is holding down the top three strings with the 3rd finger while fingers 1 and 2 hold down notes on strings 4 and 5, respectively.

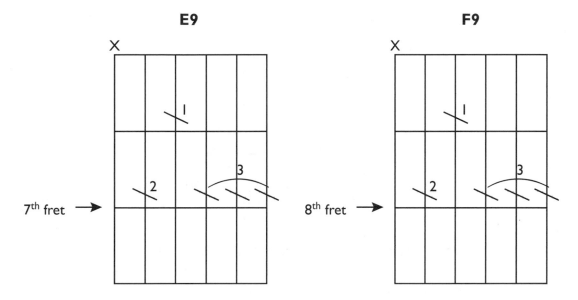

Below is a funk-style exercise using E9 and F9. The "x's" here mean release the pressure of the fingers so the notes no longer sound, then hit the strings with the pick to produce a noise of no distinct pitch. This gives a percussive effect, which is an important element in funk music.

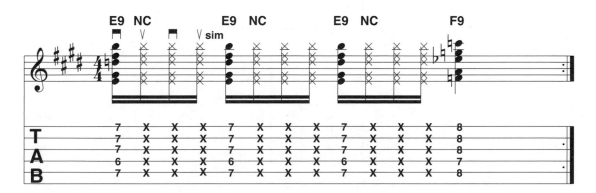

The G7sus4 Chord

This chord provides the highly distinctive intro of the Beatles' song "A Hard Day's Night." Take care to fret all the notes in the chord cleanly, particularly the *barré* note on the 4th string, which some novice players find difficult to sound clearly.

G7sus4

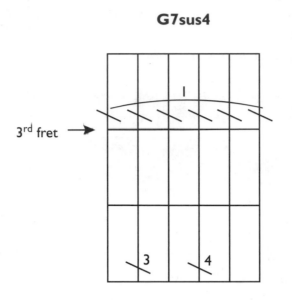

3rd fret →

No need for an exercise using G7sus4—finger the chord, hit it once, and let the notes ring on like George Harrison did!

The James Bond Chord (Em9maj7)

This highly evocative and mysterious sounding chord is played at the end of the James Bond theme:

Em9maj7

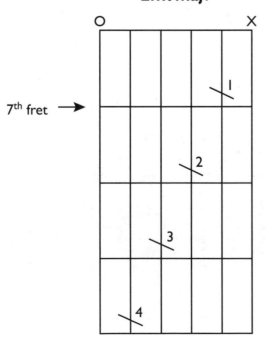

7th fret →

Again, take care to finger the notes clearly, keeping the tips of the fingers as upright as possible. As with the G7sus4 chord,

there's no need for an exercise to demonstrate this chord—just hit
it once and let the notes ring on.

The Em7, G and, Cadd9 Chords

These three chords work particularly well together and they share
the same top three notes. We've already learned the G chord but it
is included here to demonstrate this sharing of the notes on strings
1, 2, and 3.

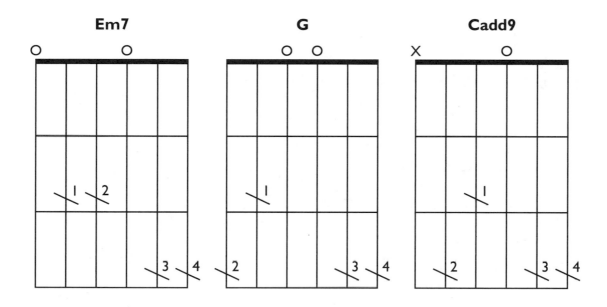

These voicings of Em7 followed by G are used for the
strummed beginning of Oasis's "Wonderwall"—with a *capo* at the
2nd fret (a *capo* is a device placed across the strings at any fret to,
in effect, raise the pitch of the open strings)—and for the picked
and strummed beginning of Pink Floyd's "Wish You Were Here,"
both intros being played on acoustic guitars.

Here's an exercise that uses these three chords:

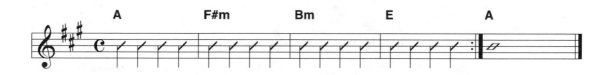

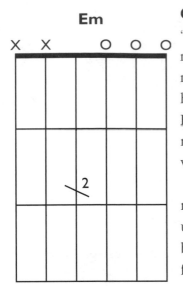

Em

Chromatic Descending Bass Line Progression

"Chromatic" means to move by one fret at a time. A standard harmonic technique is for the bass line in a chord progression in the minor key to move downwards by one fret at a time. This can be heard in many songs including Led Zeppelin's "Stairway to Heaven" and the standard "Feelings." This can be demonstrated neatly on the guitar in the key of Em, based on the four-string voicing of the basic open Em chord.

In the following exercise, notice how the bass (or lowest) note moves down one fret at a time from one bar to the next while the upper notes (the open top three strings) remain the same. This can be played with pick or fingers, the fingering showing with which fingers to pluck the strings.

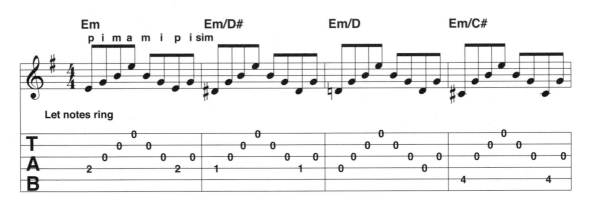

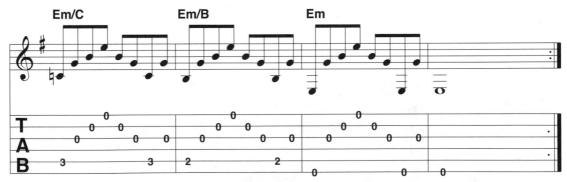

The Cycle of 5ths Progression

The cycle of 5ths progression is when the root note of a chord moves down a perfect 5th (or up a perfect 4th—it amounts to the same thing). For example, an E chord followed by an A chord. If this progression is continued, it moves through all twelve keys ending up back in the original key. Besides being an interesting chord progression, this is a useful exercise for moving around the fretboard into new keys—guitarists tend to play in the five basic open keys.

To generate a sense of movement, the following cycle of 5ths progression is all in 7th chords—remember: a 7th chord is "un-resolved" and has a restless feeling to it. This progression uses the open 7th chord shapes where possible, and if no open shape is possible a *barré* 7th chord shape has been used, formed from either the basic A7 chord shape (with the root on the 5th string) or from the basic E7 chord shape (with the root on the bottom string).

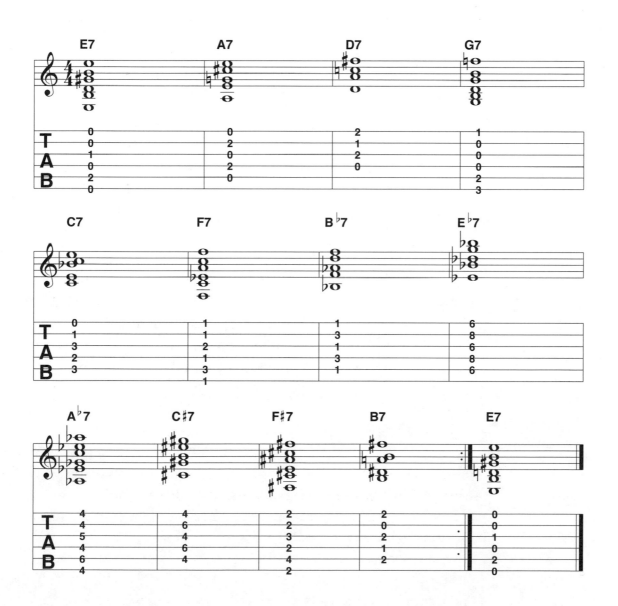

Cycle of 5ths Progression in the Minor Key

While the previous cycle of 5ths progression moved through all twelve keys, you can also get cycle of 5ths progressions that stay within the same key. Here is a cycle of 5ths in the minor key, in this case the key of A minor. This requires a Bm7♭5 chord which we covered in Chapter 9's Chord Families and Roman Numeral Chord Notation section (page 106); in case you can't remember it, here it is again. To add a touch of variety to the progression, Fmaj7 (F major 7) has been used instead of F.

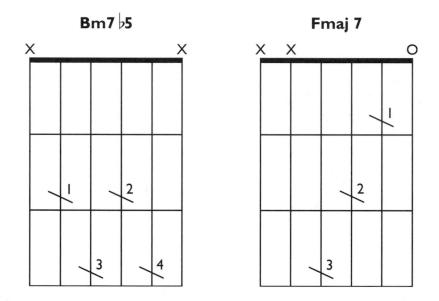

In this exercise the chords have been played as *arpeggios;* that is, by picking out one note at a time from each chord. So, simply finger each chord shape in turn and pick out the notes as required. Similar progressions can be heard in Gary Moore's "Parisienne Walkways" and the disco classic "I Will Survive."

Résumé

It is possible to play a huge number of chords on the guitar—thousands. In this chapter you have added some common and interesting chords to your vocabulary, and, just as important, you have played some musical examples using these chords. Knowing a chord is fine but it is important to be able to play it in a musical context.

Cycle of 5ths Progression in the Minor Key

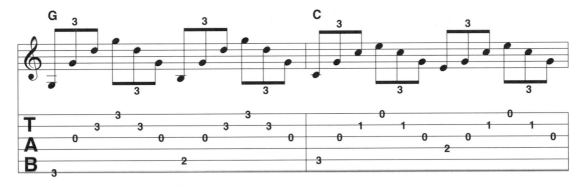

Chapter 12

Jazz

What is Jazz?

We have seen in The Twelve-Bar Blues (Chapter 5, page 45) that blues music is based on a twelve-bar chord progression with set changes. Jazz does not have an equivalent standard, typical chord progression but there are certain progressions that occur again and again, such as the II/V/I and I/VI/II/V progressions in the major key—we will look at these shortly. The most common form in jazz is a thirty-two-bar progression with an A-A-B-A structure, each of these subsections being eight bars in length. Most jazz tunes consist of a composed melody over a chord progression (the "head"); after the main melody has been played, players usually improvise over the chord progression: improvising plays an important role in jazz. Jazz is usually played with a "swing" feel, similar to the "shuffle" feel in blues.

There are several different genres of jazz with their characteristic harmonies and melodic techniques. It is difficult to sound convincing as a jazz player without immersing yourself in it. In terms of theory, jazz is a lot more complex than blues.

Chord Construction

In jazz, chords are rarely played based on just root/3rd/5th, but are often extended to include the 7th, and thus sound harmonically richer (e.g. Dm7 and Cmaj7). In order to get a percussive sound when playing them, jazz chords are often played using fretted notes only. Compare the sounds of the following chords: Dm, Dm7 using open strings, and Dm7 using fretted notes. Notice how open Dm7 sounds harmonically "richer" than Dm and how the fretted Dm7 sounds tonally "richer" than open Dm7 because it uses fretted notes instead of open strings. The fretted Dm7 involves a muted 4th string—slightly flatten the 1st finger so that it lightly touches this string resulting in a deadened note when this string is hit.

OPEN Dm

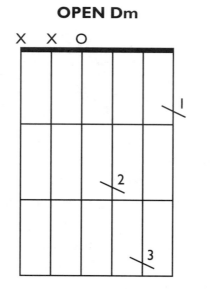

OPEN Dm7

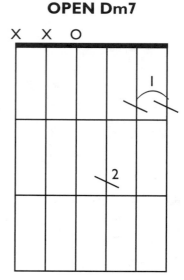

FRETTED Dm7

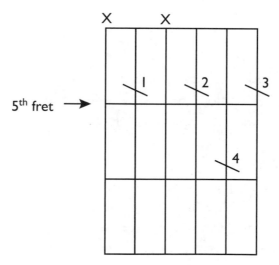

5th fret →

Similarly, compare the sounds of C, open Cmaj7, and a fretted version of Cmaj7 commonly used in jazz.

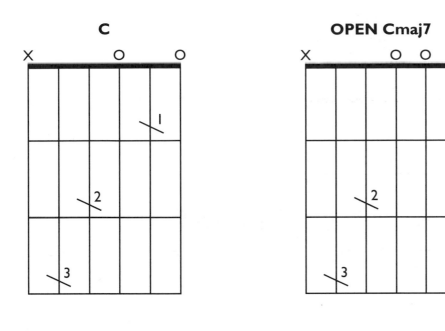

C

OPEN Cmaj7

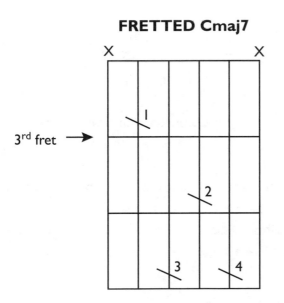

FRETTED Cmaj7

3rd fret →

The II/V/I Progression

The most common chord progression is the II/V/I in the major key—see Chapter 9 to remind yourself about Roman numeral chord notation (page 102). In the key of C this would be Dm/G7/C. Extending the minor and major chords to include the

7th changes Dm into Dm7 and C into Cmaj7. We have already learned the basic open G7, but to fit in with fretted Dm7 and Cmaj7 we need the fretted G7. Here's the basic open G7 and the fretted G7—again, compare the sounds of these chords:

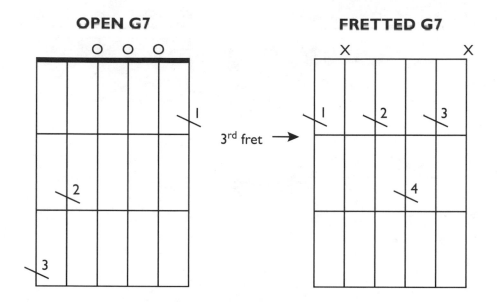

Play the following chord progression using the "fretted" versions of the chords from above, strumming each chord once:

$\frac{4}{4}$ Dm7///|G7///|Cmaj7///|Cmaj7///:||

The 7th chords sound harmonically rich, but the style of playing them doesn't sound particularly jazzy. In order to play in a jazzier style, play the chords *staccato* by relaxing the finger pressure holding down the notes as soon as the chord has been played, but don't lift the fingers from the strings. In chord slash notation, this would be written like this, the dot above each chord slash indicating a *staccato* note:

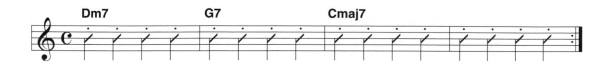

Improvising over II/V/I with Modes

There are a huge variety of melodic and harmonic techniques used by jazz soloists when improvising. The simplest is to follow the chord progression with scales. Since the Dm7, G7, and C chords are all derived from the C major scale, the C major scale can be played over all three chords. We played a one-octave C major scale in Chapter 9; here's a two-octave C major scale. Borrowing a notation device from classical guitar, the Roman numerals tell you at which fret to place the left-hand 1st finger. Keeping the fingers spread out one-finger-per-fret, this automatically determines which frets the other fingers are placed above.

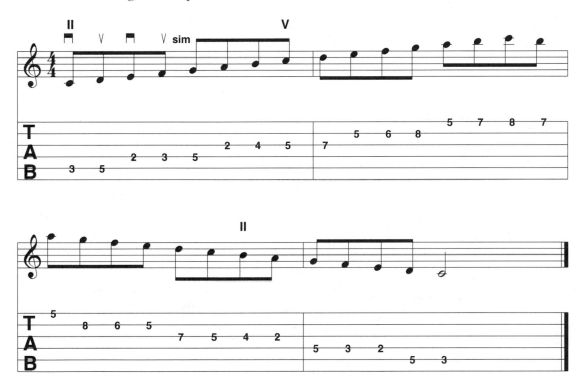

This scale will work over the chord progression. To tie in the C major scale more closely with the chords, the C major scale can be thought of in terms of modes. Think of a mode as a "scale within a scale" or a subdivision of a scale. For example, if you play the notes from the C major scale but starting from D and proceeding to the D an octave higher, you are actually playing the D Dorian mode. Similarly, if you play the C major scale from G to G you are playing the G Mixolydian mode. The C major scale, playing from C to C, is the Ionian mode. Since the C major scale contains seven different notes, a mode can be played from each of these different notes, giving rise to seven modes. Here are the seven different modes in the key of C, with the corresponding chords—this "chord scale" was covered in Chapter 9 (see page 107).

Modes in Key of 'C'

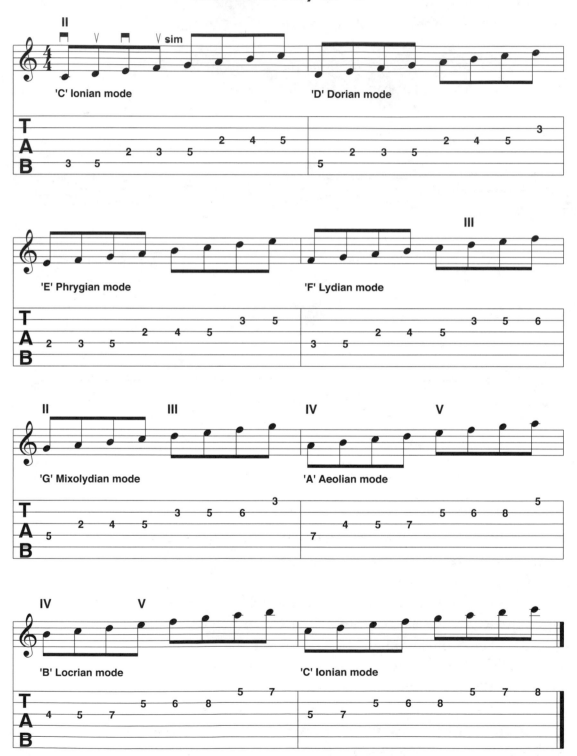

Here are the D Dorian, G Mixolydian, and C Ionian modes applied to the IIm7/V7/Imaj7 progression of Dm7/G7/C. To get a sense of how these modes work with the scales, you're going to have to play them to a tape recorder—either get a friend to play the chords or record yourself playing (remember to record a one, two, three, four count-in at the beginning so you know when to start).

Modes Applied IIm7/V7/Imaj7 in 'C'

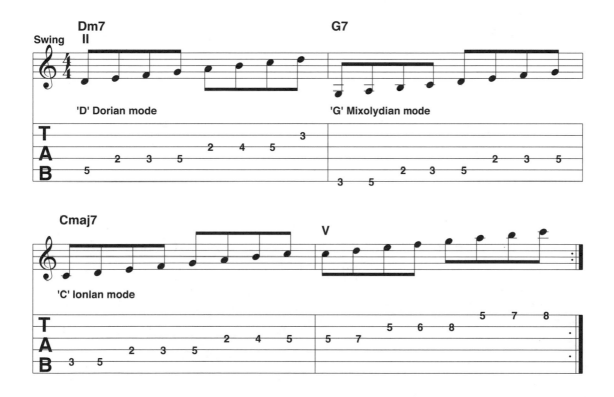

This gives a sense of how the modes fit in with the chords but it obviously doesn't sound musically interesting. Here's something more interesting over the same chord progression, again based on the modes.

Licks Over IIm7/V7/Imaj7 in 'C'

Notice the semitone slides into notes that add to the jazzy feel. The phrase over the Dm7 chord begins on a D note, but neither of the phrases over the G7 note or the Cmaj7 chord begin on G or C notes, respectively. Phrases can obviously start on any note in the mode—the modes provide a convenient way of organizing the fretboard and provide a "tonal center" from which to base one's improvising. This "tonal center" concept will become clearer at a more advanced stage and after the player has gained more experience improvising.

Improvising over II/V/I with *Arpeggios*

Another way of improvising over chords is to play *arpeggios*. Here's the IIm7/V7/Imaj7 progression outlined with *arpeggios* in *quavers*. Again, this requires playing with a friend or recording yourself on a blank tape.

Obviously this is not very interesting, musically speaking. Here's the same IIm7/V7/Imaj7 progression with a more interesting use of the corresponding *arpeggios:*

The I/VI/II/V Chord Progression

Besides the II/V/I chord progression we have already looked at, another common chord progression in jazz is the I/VI/II/V. In the key of A major this would be A/F#m/Bm/E. A and E can be played as basic open chords—you should know these!—and we learned how to form Fm and Bm *barré* chords in Chapter 8 (page 87). Here are the versions of F#m and Bm to be used in the following chord progression:

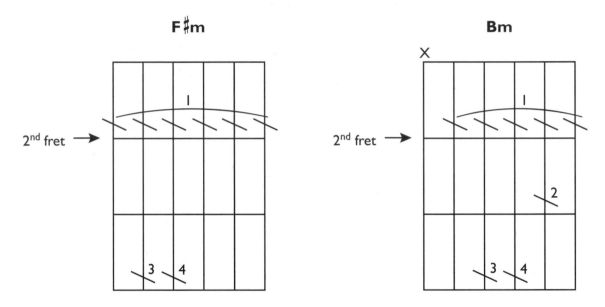

Here's the progression using these chords:

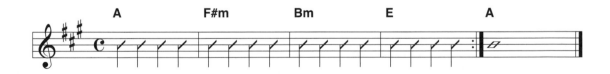

This doesn't sound particularly jazzy. To make the chords sound jazzier, they can be extended to include the 7th, giving Amaj7/F#m7/Bm7/E7. These can be fingered thus:

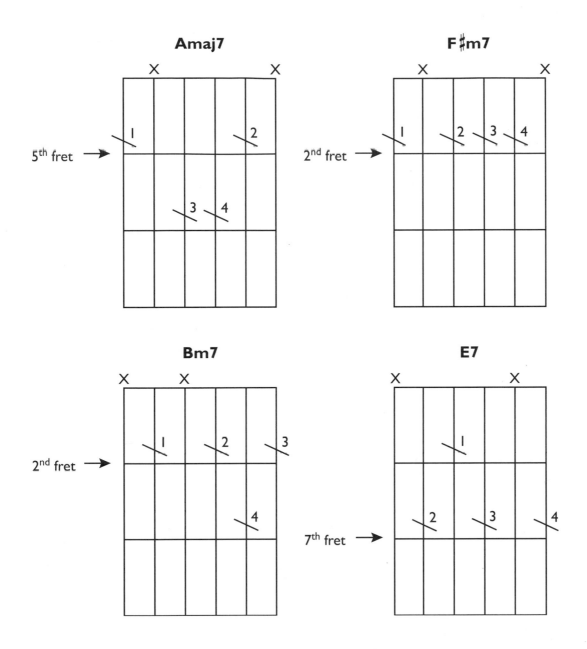

Playing the chords staccato in the same style as we treated the II/V/I chord progression earlier would be written thus:

Résumé

Again, it is worth stressing we have only touched on jazz and had a taste of what jazz music is. We have learned a new style of *staccato* accompaniment and how to apply this accompaniment to the standard jazz progressions of II/V/I and I/VI/II/V. We have learned the concept of modes and how jazz musicians play over chords using modes and *arpeggios*. The best way to get a deeper feeling for jazz is to listen to it as much as possible.

Chapter 13

Discography

The following Discography recommends guitar playing worth checking out in a variety of styles. It's intended to be inspirational and educational, although the novice player may equally feel humbled by some of the playing! Bear in mind the key words here are practice, discipline, and dedication.

All these guitarists have their own distinctive "sound" which is formed partly by their guitar and amplifier (for the electric guitarists, obviously!) but also by their particular style of playing. Of these guitarists, the ones who write the music they play also have their own characteristic harmonic and melodic traits. These factors all combine, in effect, to make their music an expression and extension of their personality.

Many of these guitarists, such as jazz guitarist John McLaughlin and classical guitarist John Williams, are extremely technically proficient and have spent literally thousands of hours of disciplined and dedicated practice to develop their style. Others, such as blues guitarist John Lee Hooker or rock 'n' roll guitarist Chuck Berry, certainly do not have technique as advanced that of McLaughlin and Williams, but that doesn't make their music any less valid, unless you're a musical snob, of course! Ultimately, music is about self-expression and communication, not about how fast or complicated someone can play.

The musical categories given below are for convenience only and some of the classifications are slightly arbitrary. As someone once said: "There are only two kinds of music—good and bad…"

This Discography is by no means exhaustive—there's loads of good guitar playing out there. Also, with many of these guitarists it's difficult to pick out just one recording. So many of them have enjoyed long careers and made many excellent recordings.

The dates given refer to the original release: all are available as original releases or re-releases.

Blues

John Lee Hooker—*John Lee Hooker Is Hip: His Greatest Hits* (2001). Hooker's trademark sound is that of accompanying himself on guitar while tapping his foot, as can be heard in "Boogie Chillen."

Robert Johnson—*The Complete Recordings* (1990). Recorded in 1936 and 1937, blues legend has it that Johnson sold his soul to the Devil in return for his guitar playing skills.

Albert King—*Born Under a Bad Sign* (1967). King played a right-handed electric guitar strung for a left-hander (so the strings were back-to-front) and he virtually wrote the book on electric guitar blues licks.

B. B. King—*Live at the Regal* (1964). No relation to Albert or Freddie, "Blues Boy" King rarely plays chords and his lead work is marked by his distinctive "hummingbird" vibrato.

Freddie King—*Let's Hide Away and Dance Away With Freddie King* (1990). King composed several blues instrumentals that became standards, such as "Hideaway" (covered by Eric Clapton with John Mayall's Bluesbreakers) and "The Stumble" (covered by Peter Green, also when with John Mayall's Bluesbreakers).

John Mayall's Bluesbreakers—*Bluesbreakers* (1966). Featuring a 21-year-old Eric Clapton, this album contains some of Clapton's fieriest playing.

John Mayall's Bluesbreakers—*A Hard Road* (1967). Replacing Clapton in the Bluesbreakers, Peter Green quickly established himself as a tasteful and expressive player.

Stevie Ray Vaughan—*Texas Flood* (1983). Vaughan updates the Albert King book of guitar licks with his huge tone and aggressive delivery.

Classical

Julian Bream—*Guitarra: The Guitar in Spain* (1985).
Bream is a very expressive player, making full use of dynamics and the tonal colors available on the classical guitar.

Andres Segovia—*Five Centuries of Spanish Guitar* (1989).
In the early 1900s, Segovia tirelessly campaigned to raise the stature of the classical guitar as a serious instrument by touring, by creating a larger repertoire for the classical guitar with his own transcriptions, and by persuading contemporary composers to write for the instrument.

John Williams—*The Seville Concert* (1993).
A very precise and technically flawless player, in this recording Williams performs many standard pieces from the classical guitar repertoire.

Country

Chet Atkins—*The Early Years of Chet Atkins and His Guitar* (1964).
An accomplished fingerpicker, Atkins once commented: "Merle Travis and I pretty much taught America how to fingerpick."

Albert Lee—*Speechless* (1986).
Lee is a renowned session musician who has played with Jerry Lee Lewis, Emmylou Harris, the Everly Brothers, and many others. This instrumental album demonstrates his formidable technique on both electric and acoustic guitar.

Merle Travis—*Walkin' the Strings* (1960).
Along with Chet Atkins, Travis is a hugely influential fingerpicker and even has a style of picking named after him: "Travis picking."

Flamenco

Paco de Lucia—*Luzia* (1999).
De Lucia pushes back the boundaries of traditional flamenco with new harmonies and techniques, executed with formidable technique.

Juan Martin—*Andalucian Suites* (1998).
Martin specializes in Andalucian traditions of flamenco and wrote the acclaimed flamenco guitar tutor book *El Arte Flamenco de la Guitarra*.

Paco Peña—*The Flamenco World of Paco Peña* (1978).
A traditionalist and expert flamenco guitarist, Peña sees his role to preserve and promote traditional flamenco culture.

Folk

Davy Graham—*Folk, Blues and Beyond* (1964).
An eclectic mixture of folk, blues, jazz, and baroque influences, Graham took the acoustic guitar into new territory.

Bert Jansch—*Jack Orion* (1966).
Jansch reworks traditional folk forms and duets on four tracks with John Renbourn.

John Renbourn—*The Hermit* (1973).
Mixing classical and folk influences with jazz and even Middle Eastern inflections, Renbourn's style is often called "folk-baroque."

Richard Thompson—*Watching the Dark* (1993).
A former member of folk-rock pioneers' Fairport Convention, Thompson fuses many diverse musical influences on this career history, which shows him equally comfortable and distinctive on both acoustic and electric guitar.

Jazz

Charlie Christian—*Solo Flight* (1941).
A pioneer of the electric guitar, Christian showed the electric guitar had a place as a lead instrument in jazz bands and helped take jazz from the swing era into bop.

Al DiMeola—*Elegant Gypsy* (1977).
As much rock as jazz—or fusion, if you will—DiMeola displays formidable pick technique on electric and acoustic guitar.

John McLaughlin—*Extrapolation* (1969).
An extremely technically accomplished player and a very intense player, McLaughlin is persistently striving for new means of expression.

Wes Montgomery—*The Incredible Jazz Guitar of Wes Montgomery* (1960).
> Montgomery's dexterity with octaves made them a standard part of the guitarists' vocabulary.

Joe Pass—*Virtuoso* (1973).
> Solo improvisations on jazz standards: Pass improvises chords, melody, and bass lines simultaneously.

Django Reinhardt—*The Classic Early Recordings* (2000).
> A master improviser, Reinhardt's solos were endlessly inventive and usually played with wild abandon.

Rock

Jeff Beck—*Beckology* (1992).
> Arguably the most consistent rock guitarist, this compilation demonstrates that Beck has been inventive and distinctive throughout his long musical career.

Cream—*Wheels of Fire* (1968).
> This is a partly live album. With Eric Clapton on lead guitar, Cream took improvising in a rock band to new heights, as heard on the live reinterpretation of Robert Johnson's *Crossroads*.

Deep Purple—*Made In Japan* (1972).
> Responsible for "Smoke on the Water," one of the best-known guitar riffs, Purple guitarist Ritchie Blackmore claims to be one of rock's best improvisers, as demonstrated on this live recording.

Dire Straits—*Money for Nothing* (1988).
> This "greatest hits" package showcases Mark Knopfler's highly distinctive sound of fingerpicking on a clean-toned Stratocaster guitar.

Jimi Hendrix—*Are You Experienced?* (1967).
> Hendrix is credited with inventing the vocabulary of the electric guitar, harnessing distortion and feedback in a musical melting pot of blues, rock, and R&B.

Led Zeppelin—*Remasters* (1990).
> This compilation demonstrates Jimmy Page's diverse talents on electric and acoustic guitars, as well as his arranging skills, best demonstrated in "Stairway to Heaven."

Metallica—*Metallica* (1991).
> The polished production, use of dynamics (listen to the opener "Enter Sandman"), and Kirk Hammett's bluesy soloing brought a new diversity and depth to Metallica's sound and propelled them into the mainstream.

Yngwie Malmsteen—*Rising Force* (1984).
> Malmsteen's mixture of classical influences and heavy rock is an acquired taste, although as a guitarist you can't help but marvel at his technique—breathtakingly agile scale runs and *arpeggios,* rounded off with a dramatic *vibrato.*

Police—*Regatta De Blanc* (1979).
> Andy Summer's innovative yet subtle use of effects inspired a school of "texturalist" guitarists.

Queen—*Greatest Hits* (1981).
> This album demonstrates Brian May's sweet tone, use of harmonies, and an instinctive ability to tailor his playing to suit the song.

Santana—*The Ultimate Collection* (1998).
> A very soulful player, Santana mixes rock, Latin, and blues influences.

Joe Satriani—*Surfing With The Alien* (1987).
> Accessible instrumental rock played with virtuosity and taste from the teacher of Metallica's Kirk Hammett and Steve Vai.

Steve Vai—*Passion & Warfare* (1990).
> With a fertile musical imagination and formidable technique, Vai takes instrumental rock into new territories.

Van Halen—*Van Halen I* (1978).
> Eddie Van Halen reinvented the electric guitar with right-hand tapping, pinch harmonic squeals, and *vibrato* arm abuse—after Hendrix, the second most important and influential electric rock guitarist.

Yes—*The Yes Album* (1971).
> Guitarist Steve Howe is one of the few rock guitarists who is not obviously blues-based, instead showing classical, jazz, and country influences—*The Yes Album* features Howe's signature acoustic instrumental: "Clap."

Rock 'n' Roll

Chuck Berry—*The Great Twenty-Eight* (1984).
Berry was an innovator, mixing country, blues, and jump-jive influences and forging his own unique style. Not the most precise of guitarists—on some of these tracks he doesn't even play in tune!—but he still sounds great.

Gene Vincent—*The EP Collection* (1989).
Vincent's guitarist—Cliff Gallup—is much overlooked, but his sophisticated playing inspired many players including Albert Lee and Jeff Beck.

Soul

Booker T. and The MG's—*Green Onions* (1962).
Although the guitar is not normally a particularly prominent instrument in soul, Steve Cropper's contribution as a member of Booker T. and The MG's (the Stax label house band) cannot be underestimated, having made significant contributions to recordings by Otis Reading, Eddie Floyd, and many others.

Afterword

So, now that you have come this far, where to go from here? While self-tuition is undeniably rewarding and an exciting voyage of self-discovery, in the longer term there's no substitute for a good teacher. A good teacher can correct subtle but important points of technique that you may have overlooked, and can provide suitable music to help you make faster progress than if teaching yourself.

Finding a teacher can be a tricky process, and the best players don't necessarily make the best teachers. A personal recommendation from a friend or colleague is a good guide; otherwise, music shops often have lists of teachers and some teachers advertise locally. Most teachers will happily provide a one-off initial lesson to assess your ability; this also gives the chance for you to assess the teacher. It's important for teacher and pupil to be compatible and to develop a rapport. A teacher/pupil relationship is a two-way street, as it were, and if you tell the teacher where you want to go, the teacher can help you get there.

As far as other teaching materials are concerned, guitarists have never been better served. Gone are the days when Paul McCartney was learning the guitar: "We'd take bus rides for hours to visit the guy who knew B7!" There are hundreds of specialized guitar tuition books, videos, and magazines available.

Playing along to a metronome is an invaluable way to improve your timing; when practicing on your own it's all too easy to speed up on the easy bits and slow down when you come to a difficult chord change or tricky passage. A metronome will help you achieve a constant tempo all the way through. It's also a good idea to play with other people—this is another way to improve your sense of timing. Playing with people better than yourself will also help to improve your playing.

There are several graded series of exams for both classical and electric guitar, set by various examining bodies. Graded exams give candidates something to aim for, a sense of achievement (assuming they pass!), and a concrete way of measuring progress.

Also, because of the way they are structured, they encourage a well-rounded musical ability: most exams involve performing prescribed pieces, scales and *arpeggios,* sight reading, and ear tests. But equally, music exams are not for everyone. Remember, whatever path you choose, playing the guitar—and any musical instrument for that matter—should be fun! Good luck!

Glossary

The following glossary is aimed at beginners; at an intermediate and/or advanced level many of the terms merit fuller explanations.

Acciaccatura—a grace note played as quickly as possible before the main note.

Accidentals—sharps or flats or naturals in a piece of music outside the key signature.

Action—the distance between the strings and the fingerboard/fretboard of a guitar.

Apoyando—a rest stroke, whereby after plucking the string the (plucking) finger comes to rest on the next string.

Arpeggio—the notes of a chord played one at a time.

Barré—a technique used in fingering chords whereby the 1st finger of the left hand lies across all six strings of the guitar.

Bars—"chunks" of written music, indicated by vertical lines (bar lines) that break the music down into bars.

Body—the "bulky" part of any guitar, as distinct from the neck.

Bridge—the part of the guitar on the body that the strings rest on.

Bottom string—the string that sounds the lowest in pitch, string 6 or bottom E.

C—as a time signature, this means "common time" which is $\frac{4}{4}$

Capo—short for *capotasto;* a device that is fastened across the strings to, in effect, raise the pitch of the open strings.

Chord—two or more notes played simultaneously.

Chromatic—moving one fret at a time.

Concert pitch—an internationally accepted standard pitch that enables instruments to be tuned at the same pitch.

Diatonic—containing no sharps or flats outside the key.

Dissonant—a musical "clash" between notes.

Double dots—two dots at the end of a bar in a piece of music mean repeat from the beginning or from the previous pair of double dots at the beginning of a bar.

Double-bar lines—in a piece of written music two bar lines instead of a single-bar line mean the end of a section. A thin line followed by a thick line means end of the piece.

End pin—the metal protrusion on the bottom of an electric or acoustic guitar that a strap attaches over.

Fermata—a pause sign consisting of a semi-circle curled around a dot, indicating the player should pause at this point in the music.

Fingerboard/fretboard—the part of the neck with the frets, on which the left-hand fingers are placed to finger notes.

Flat—(1) A flat sign in music lowers a note in pitch by one fret. (2) To say "that note is slightly flat" means that the note is slightly low.

Free stroke—also known as *tirando,* a plucking technique in which after plucking a string the finger moves over the next string.

Frets—the lengths of metal on the fretboard that the left-hand fingers are placed behind in order to finger a note.

Hammer-on—a technique whereby a note is sounded by bringing a finger of the left hand firmly down on the string causing the note to sound without needing to be plucked by the right hand.

Head/headstock—the opposite end of the guitar from the body at the end of the neck on which the machine heads are mounted.

Jack plug socket—the part of the electric guitar where a jack is plugged in, the other end of the guitar lead being plugged into an amplifier.

Key—a key is the scale that a piece of music is based on that determines which chords are used in the piece.

Key signature—the arrangement of sharps or flats between the treble clef and the time signature that determines which key the piece of music is in.

Ledger lines—the short lines above and below the stave that extend the range of the stave.

Let notes ring—a direction to give notes longer than their notated value by letting them ring on until they die away naturally.

Lick—a short melodic phrase in blues, rock, jazz, and country music.

Machine heads/tuning machines—the six mechanical devices on the head/headstock of the guitar that are turned to tune the strings.

Metronome—a clockwork or electric device that can be set to click at various speeds to enable the musician to play at the required tempo.

Modes—a "scale within a scale"; the major scale consists of seven notes—starting the scale on each of these seven notes in turn and proceeding to the same note an octave higher produces seven different modes.

Movable chords—a chord consisting solely of fretted notes, which means it can be moved up and/or down the fretboard while remaining the same type of chord.

Natural—a sign in a piece of music that cancels out a sharp or flat.

NC—No Chord. A direction that no chord shape is to be held down by the left hand.

Neck—the long, thin part of the guitar attached to the bulkier body.

Nut—the piece of plastic where the headstock joins the fretboard that the strings pass through by means of appropriately sized slots.

Octave—the musical "gap" or "interval" of eight scale notes or twelve chromatic notes, starting with, say, an A note and ending on the next A note; the distance between the open 5th string, A, and the note on the 5th string 12th fret, also A, is an octave.

Open string—the note produced from any string when no left-hand finger is placed on the fretboard.

Palm muting—a technique whereby the palm of the right hand is lightly rested on the strings close to the bridge, thereby altering the tone and producing a "chunky" sound.

Partial *barré*—a chord in which a finger, normally the 1st finger, holds down two, three, four, or five strings at the same fret.

Pick guard/scratch plate—the piece of plastic on the body of an acoustic or electric guitar that protects the guitar from pick scratches.

Pick ups—the arrangement of magnets on the body of an electric guitar that "pick up" the sound.

Pick—the piece of shaped plastic used by acoustic and electric guitarists to pluck the strings.

Position—(1) In classical guitar, playing in the 5th position means the 1st finger is at the 5th fret, which determines which frets the other fingers are poised above. (2) In blues, the "1st position blues scale" is a particular pattern of the blues scale that can be played at any fret.

Power chord—a chord consisting of root and 5th. Power chords have a "bare" sound since they are neither major nor minor and sound particularly effective when played with distortion.

Pull-off—a technique whereby a note is sounded by pulling a left-hand finger off the fretboard after plucking the fretted note, causing the note to sound without needing to be plucked by the right hand.

Quaver—a tremulous sound, such as a trill produced on an instrument; also a musical note having the time value of an eighth of a whole note.

Relative tuning method—a method of tuning the guitar that enables it to be in tune with itself, even though it may not be at concert pitch.

Rest stroke—see *Apoyando*.

Riff—a short series of repeated notes or chords, often in the low register, which are usually played at the beginning of a song then repeated at other points. Most rock songs are based on guitar riffs.

Roman numerals—(1) In chord notation, a Roman numeral refers to which note of the scale the chord is built on, which determines the type of chord, that is, whether it is major or minor, etc. (2) In classical guitar fingering, a Roman numeral tells the player at which fret to place the 1st finger, and determines which frets the other fingers are poised above.

Root—the first note of a scale; the note in a chord—the lowest note in the case of most basic chords—on which the chord is built.

Scale—a gradually ascending or descending series of notes; in the seven-note major scale each letter name appears once and once only.

Sharp—(1) A sharp sign in music raises a note in pitch by one fret. (2) To say "that note is slightly sharp" means that the note is slightly high.

Shuffle—a rhythm used in blues in which the first *quaver* of each pair of *quavers* is lengthened and the second is shortened, resulting in a "duuh-da, duuh-da" rhythm.

Sim—short for "simile" meaning continue in a similar manner.

Slash chord—a chord name such as C/E which means a C chord played over an E bass note; normally a C chord has a C note in the bass.

Slide—a technique where a left-hand finger is slid from one note to another, thereby sounding all the notes in between.

Slur—a curved line joining two notes of different pitches indicating the second of the two notes is not to be plucked; rather, it is sounded by sliding to, pulling-off to, or hammering-on to.

Sound box—the hollow body of an acoustic or classical guitar that acts as an amplifier and shapes the tone of the guitar.

Soundboard—the top of an acoustic or classical guitar that, as part of the sound box, helps to amplify the sound and shape the tone.

Sound hole—the hole in the sound box of an acoustic or classical guitar from where the sound emanates.

Staccato—the shortening of a note for musical effect, indicated by a dot above or below the note.

Stave—or staff, the five lines on which music is written.

Straight 8s—when pairs of *quavers* are played equally, as opposed to the shuffle or swing rhythms.

Strap pin—the metal protrusion on the body of the guitar near the neck over which a strap attaches.

Swing—the rhythmic feel in jazz in which the first *quaver* of each pair of *quavers* is lengthened and the second *quaver* is shortened.

Tablature—a method of notating guitar music in which six lines represent the six strings, top line representing top string and bottom line representing bottom string, with numbers written on the lines telling the player which frets to play.

Ties—curved lines that join two notes of the same pitch, meaning the note gets the combined value of both notes.

Time signature—the two numbers at the beginning of music; the top number tells the number of beats in the bar and the bottom number tells the value of each beat, that is, what type of note is being used to represent the beat.

Tirando—a free stroke, whereby after plucking the string the finger moves over the top of the next string.

Treble clef—the "squiggly" sign at the beginning of a piece of music, the start of which determines the position of G on the second bottom line of the stave.

Top string—the string that sounds the highest in pitch, string 1 or top E.

Triad—a chord consisting of three notes: the root, 3rd, and 5th.

Triplet—three notes played in the space of one beat.

Turnaround—a progression found in the last two bars of a twelve-bar blues that rounds off the previous ten bars and prepares for the next twelve bars.

***Vibrato* arm**—the bar on some electric guitars that is attached to the bridge, used to waver the notes in pitch.

Voicing—the particular arrangement of notes that make up a chord; every chord can be played in different ways by rearranging the notes, each rearrangement being a different voicing.

Volume and tone controls—the rotary knobs on an electric guitar that alter the guitar's volume and tone.

Index

Twelve-bar blues, 45–60
  boogie/boogie variations riffs, 57–60
  jazz/blues bass riff, 55–56
  shuffle blues in E, 46–52
  shuffle variations, 52–54
"Twinkle Twinkle Little Star" (Green & Taylor), 26, 27

U
Ultimate Collection (Santana), 148
"Unchained Melody," 75

V
Vai, Steve, 148
Van Halen, Eddie, 148
Van Halen I (Van Halen), 148
Vaughan, Stevie Ray, 144
Vibrato arm, 5

Vincent, Gene, 149
Virtuoso (Pass), 147
Voicings, 92–93, 99
Volume/tone controls, 5

W
Walkin' the Strings (Travis), 145
Waltz time, 34
Watching the Dark (Thompson), 146
Wheels of Fire (Cream), 147
"Wild Thing" (Troggs), 86
Williams, John, 2, 143, 145
"Wish You Were Here" (Pink Floyd), 125
"Wonderwall" (Oasis), 6, 125
Wrist, strains in, 2

Y
Yes Album (Yes), 148

787.8719 Noble, Douglas J.
NOB
       The beginner's guide
       to playing guitar.

                                    262476

$12.95

DATE			
AG 1 0 '05			
JA 1 0 06			
JE 0 5 '06			
FE 2 6 07			
FHR 1 4 2008			
OCT 2 6 2010			
JAN 1 3 2012			

HERITAGE PUB LIBY
RTE 155 & 629
PROVIDENCE FORGE VA
          23140
07/07/2005

BAKER & TAYLOR